P9-AEU-696

BUILDING A CORPORATE INTERNET STRATEGY

Other VNR Business Technology/Communications Books.....

10263

BUILDING A CORPORATE INTERNET STRATEGY

THE IT MANAGER'S GUIDE

AMIT K. MAITRA

I(T)P® A Division of International Thomson Publishing Inc.

New York • Albany • Bonn • Boston • Detroit • London • Madrid • Melbourne
Mexico City • Paris • San Francisco • Singapore • Tokyo • Toronto

TRADEMARKS

The words contained in this text which are believed to be trademarked, service marked, or otherwise to hold proprietary rights have been designated as such by use of initial capitalization. No attempt has been made to designate as trademarked or service marked any personal computer words or terms in which proprietary rights might exist. Inclusion, exclusion, or definition of a word or term is not intended to affect, or to express judgment upon, the validity of legal status of any proprietary right which may be claimed for a specific word or term.

Copyright © 1996 by Van Nostrand Reinhold

I(T)P ™ Van Nostrand Reinhold is a division of International Thomson Publishing, Inc.
The ITP logo is a trademark under license

Printed in the United States of America

For more information, contact:

Van Nostrand Reinhold
115 Fifth Avenue
New York, N.Y. 10003

International Thomson Publishing
GmbH
Königswinterer Strasse 418
353227 Bonn
Germany

International Thomson Publishing Europe
Berkshire House 168-173
High Holborn
London WCIV 7AA
England

International Thomson Publishing Asia
221 Henderson Road #05-10
Henderson Building
Singapore 0315

Thomas Nelson Australia
102 Dodds Street
South Melbourne, 3205
Victoria, Australia

International Thomson Publishing Japan
Hirakawacho Kyowa Building, 3F
2-2-1 Hirakawacho
Chiyoda-ku, 102 Tokyo
Japan

Nelson Canada
1120 Birchmount Road
Scarborough, Ontario
Canada M1K 5G4

International Thomson Editores
Seneca 53
Col. Polanco
11560 Mexico D.F. Mexico

All rights reserved. No part of this work covered by the copyright hereon may be
reproduced or used in any form or by any means—graphic, electronic, or mechanical, including photocopying, recording, taping, or information storage and retrieval systems—without the written permission of the publisher.

1 2 3 4 5 6 7 8 9 10 QEBFF 02 01 00 99 98 97 96

Library of Congress Cataloging-in-Publication Data
Maitra, Amit.
    Building a corporate internet strategy: the it manager's guide/
by Amit Maitra.
      p.   cm
    Includes bibliographical references and index.
    ISBN 0-442-02246-8
    1. Business enterprises—Computer networks--Management.
  2. Information technology--Management. 3. Internet (Computer
network) 4. World Wide servers. I. Title
    HD30.37.M35   1996
    658' .05467--dc20   96-19588
                                                        CIP

To Julie
and
My Parents

Contents

Preface

A fundamental change is taking place in the nature and application of the Internet in business. This change has profound and far-reaching implications for your organization and for you. Most enterprises, large and small, are rushing, dollars in hand, to fund a plethora of seemingly promising Internet projects. But what are these enterprises really funding?

There is much more to the art of using the Internet to gain a competitive toehold than just a mere E-Mail application or home page on a Web site for advertising purposes. The Internet, driven by demands of the new, competitive business environment, is forcing enterprises to integrate data, text, voice, and image information in various formats, and also to be open and networked. It is dynamic—based on interchangeable parts—and it technologically empowers by distributing decision making to users in all functions, including marketing, customer service, human resources, security and legal, as well as traditional technical experts within the information services division of the enterprise. The Internet is providing a backbone for team-oriented business structures. A shift is occurring in the nature of enterprises and how they gather, maintain, use, and update their data and information.

The motivation for this book is really quite simple. Its intention is to make the enterprise decision makers aware of the Internet paradox: massive funding of the home page construction for a possible Web site for advertising, interactive marketing, customer support, and processing electronic transactions do not necessarily translate into higher efficiency, productivity, or return on investments (ROI). Rather, enterprises that are currently adopting and endorsing an interactive and consolidated network environment for the entire operation of their organizations will move ahead at a more rapid pace than those that aren't. These two factors—interaction and consolidation—form the basis for achieving success through the Internet.

Information accessed by a user through a home page on the Internet can cover all operations and divisions of an enterprise and can even extend to externally produced data. Online information services via electronic mail networks allow interactions with the information areas relative to financial data, energy loads, safety performance, and any other type of productivity data. The onus is on the executive management of a given enterprise to internally maintain and also to present to the outside world a consolidated view of the organization. To ensure that the enterprise's service offerings are promoted accurately and clearly, and that the information is refreshed in a timely manner, the management must take strategic steps to stay on top of everything that is being reported by the people about the organization. Herein lies the need for the enterprisewide policy and/or procedural framework to make clear certain cases which are consistent with the business objectives of a given enterprise. Appropriate policy guidance will help plug the administrative "holes" that are usually present in an organization's use of authorization, maintenance, and responsibility for enterprise data and information.

This book investigates the critical enterprise integration policy and procedural dimensions necessary to help you uncover the new promise of the Internet in your organization. It provides a framework for deriving ROI based on, among other things, "soft" benefits. Additionally, this framework offers your enterprise fresh insight on how to use the Internet to provide a positive presence within the organization.

Amit K. Maitra

Acknowledgments

As a first-time author, I would like to acknowledge individuals who formed the direct chain leading to the publishing of this book. First of all, I would like to thank my wife Julie, for providing the moral support that I needed in order to devote a substantial period of my life to this endeavor. Second, I want to acknowledge my indebtedness to USAir Information Services Division for giving me the opportunity to discover, experiment with, struggle with, and grow in understanding of Internet technologies. I would not be where I am today were it not for the assignments I had received to define a USAir strategy which involved evolution to an enterprise Internet, based on the Internet technologies, for achieving the overall USAir vision. In particular, I wish to acknowledge the support of Jack Cowan, senior director of coordination, technology, and infrastructure development, Bob Crafts, senior director, marketing, applications development, and Nicholas Doggett, manager, technical architecture, USAir information services division.

USAir connected to the Internet in 1994 via a Unix dial-up connect service. By early 1995, it was apparent that there was a need to undertake a joint effort with users and Corporate Information Services to define a comprehensive strategy and vision for the USAir Internet network infrastructure and user guidelines. Because USAir is a consensus-driven company, Jack Cowan and Nicholas Doggett initially asked me to drive an effort to expose the Internet throughout the corporation and then develop a plan of action that would ensure participation and buy-in from as diverse a group of network stakeholders and users as possible. Without the vision and insight of Jack Cowan, Bob Crafts, and Nicholas Doggett, the USAir Enterprisewide Internet Strategy Development effort would not have gotten underway.

The whole exercise on Internet deployment at USAir proved to be very timely, productive, and worthwhile. Having seen the need for this book early in the Internet deployment efforts at USAir, I was fortunate that Neil Levine of Van Nostrand Reinhold (VNR) suggested that I send him a proposal for the book. As there was no book covering the topic thoroughly, I wrote the first draft for VNR.

Several people made contributions to the actual development of this book. I would like to acknowledge the superb professionalism—not to mention the patience and understanding—shown by Rick Smith, executive vice president, and Jason Bott at Interpath. They taught me the basics of the Internet technology at a time when my knowledge in the field was virtually nonexistent.

I want to acknowledge all the other people who contributed to the structuring of the methods and frameworks presented in this book. I am acquainted with only some of you, but learning about your thoughts or work has allowed me to articulate methods through which, I believe, other Enterprisewide Internet Strategy successes will be achieved. I want to mention: Jim Boland (CIO), John Harper (CFO), John Fair, Ross Cotjanle, Jo Ann Sliwa, Ralph Marshal, Howard Grams, and Bill Demarest at USAir; Victor Wheatman, B. Enslow, A. Pasik, J. Popkin, B. Reilly, E. Stear, D. Taylor, and M. Zboray at Gartner Group; Thomas Rheinlander, H. Waverly Deutsch, George F. Colony, Paul D. Callahan, Anne E. Trenkle at Forrester Research; Ira Chaleff at The Institute for Business Technology; Richard Drummond at Drummond Group; Steven Pliskin at Deloitte & Touche Management Consulting; Paul J. Dravis at J.P. Morgan Equities Research; John Coviello at American Airlines Sabre Computer Services; Suzanne M. Johnson at Intel Corporation; Laura Poe and Eugene Leonardi at Sun Microsystems; John Patrick and Nicholas R. Trio at IBM; Walter Okon and Kimberly Barron at the Defense Information Systems Agency; Albert J. Simone at the University of Hawaii; Rex E. Lee, Sterling J. Albrecht, and Douglas M. Chabries at Brigham Young University; H. S. Peter Jones and Ken R. Maharaj at Dalhousie University; Philip H. Jordan, Jr., Paul Gherman, and Thomas Moberg at Kenyon College; Pamela S. MacBrayne, Thomas E. Abbott, Fred Hurst, and Robert S. Tolsma at the University of Maine; Linda Deneen at the University of Minnesota; James J. Duderstadt, Douglas E. Van Houweling, Donald E. Riggs, and Michael J. McGill at the University of Michigan; David Lytel at the Office of Science and Technology Policy; Jerry Mulvenna and Mark Mandell at the National Institute of Standards and Technology; Ernest Daddio at the National Oceanic and Atmospheric Administration; Frank Campbell and Michael Fitzmaurice at the Department of Health and Human Services; Ken Buckley at the Board of Governors of the Federal Reserve System; Robert Anderson and Paul Grant at the Department of Defense; Donald Josephs at the Department of Justice; Nancy Correia at the Department of Transportation; Louise Murphy at the Federal Communications Commission; Rosetta Bowsky at the Federal Emergency Management; Charmayne Parks and Michael Corrigan at the General Services Administration; Sherrie S. Aly of the Office of the Joint Chiefs of Staff; Tony Villasenor and John Mathews at National Aeronautics and Space Administration; Ken Heist at National Security Agency; and Alan Proctor at the Federal Trade Commission.

To each and every one of you: Thank you.

Introduction

THE SCOPE OF THIS BOOK

There are more than 150 books in publication today that contain "Internet," or a related term such as "Intranet" or the World Wide Web or Gopher in their titles. The challenge for enterprises that want to make use of the Internet as a business tool or resource is to narrow down the choices to one book that contains everything from a strategy for developing business policies concerning marketing, selling, facilitating markets, and disseminating information on the Internet to setting up Web servers with restrictions on enterprise communications issues, research, browsing, downloading, other inbound data activities, and security. Don't worry, be happy. You found the book! **This is that book.**

The focus of this work is on goal-setting for Internet and Intranet technology investments: what principles help you examine a proposal for changing systems that manage an organization. By focusing on where, when, and how to make management more productive by Internet/Intranet connections, Enterprisewide Internet Strategies gives you effective and practical strategies for measuring management productivity, which Paul Strassmann, the twenty-first century consultant and former CIO of the Department of Defense, emphasizes as the key to knowing how to invest in information technologies.

Each chapter is packed full of useful, usable intelligence including detailed case studies that will give you an inside look at how other companies are using the Internet to gather information, promote their products, and generate new business. You will learn how to:

- link the spending to business goals; determine nonquantifiable intangible benefits; and capture anticipated numbers that are watched and understood by your board of directors, your top executives, and your shareholders;

- develop an Internet policy that allows for effective use of the medium by all areas within your company—from research and development and information systems management to marketing, legal, customer service, and human resources;

- "put your best foot forward" on the Internet by creating a presence that generates attention while accurately depicting your company's philosophy, products, and people;

- monitor your Internet connection to ensure the integrity of the information that is going out and coming in.

The Internet and its special application, the Intranet, can be your company's key to success now and in the future but only if you know how to use it to your particular advantage. Above and beyond the critical factors identified above, this book will provide an additional input. It will delineate how to achieve consistent high performance by using the Internet as a convenient mechanism for interdepartmental exchange of information and partnership with other outside organizations in providing information based services both to the business community and the public.

AUDIENCE

This book is aimed at business decision makers—CEOs, CFOs, and CIOs who want to make informed judgements about the Internet, including its special application, the Intranet, as a key enabling technology that could improve the efficiency and effectiveness of enterprise business. Project and technical managers will equally benefit from a better understanding of the overall business requirements of facilitating interoperability between Internet and the Intranet information services. These project and technical managers will eventually guide enterprises in developing, specifying, and aligning the plethora of Internet information tools into a single, virtually unified information service. Having noted that, it is important to clarify a point: this book is not directed at systems engineers or programmers who are creating Enterprise Internet by designing and implementing TCP/IP (Transmission Control Protocol/Internet Protocol[1]) routing architectures and infrastructures and attendant security features. These things are essential in setting and implementing effective Internet/Intranet services, but this book leaves treatment of those issues is better left to other sources.

THE ORGANIZATION OF THIS BOOK

This book departs from the usual presentation style of other available Internet books, which describe the various solutions and then propose some techniques to get your business moving in that direction. This book is meant to be a starting place for further investigation and should be viewed as a useful resource in terms of:

---

[1] These will be defined in chapter 2.

- WHAT could be done with the Internet and the Intranet? Hypothetical applications identify the possibilities.

- HOW could you do it? Electronic Mail (E-mail), File Transfer Protocol (FTP), World Wide Web (WWW).

- WHY should you do it? Return On Investment/Return On Management.

- WHO takes care of the administrative procedures? Enterprise Internet Policy Directive.

- WHERE are the good results? Case histories of real life experiences of the Internet as a mass interactive communications tool and its marketing might.

For a business to do well with the Internet and the Intranet, the technology must be clearly understood. Accordingly, chapter 1 provides conceptual information about E-mail, FTP, WWW, etc., and explains how each tool works and how the tool is used in the Internet community with the appropriate addition of [embedded or external] security features.

Chapter 2 explores Internet's impact on business and the people the particular enterprise serves. In so doing, chapter 3 generates and documents a set of business needs and agenda.

Chapter 3 reduces those needs to develop and justify the functional and performance requirements for linking the enterprise. We need to be clear and precise on our understanding of the phrase "functional and performance requirements," and how it is different from the purely technical requirements.

Given the fact that the Internet, and its associated application Intranet, is a new medium, an enterprise must develop new strategies to utilize it. "New strategies" mean different things to different people. For instance, IBM has announced an Enterprise Internet Initiative that will enable large, medium, and small companies to integrate the Internet into their computing infrastructures [1]. This initiative is a comprehensive service option available to a company in order to implement Internet components that enable "standard" interfaces to E-mail, FTP, Telnet, Mosaic with the Worldwide Web (WWW), USENET News (25,000+ users groups), and Internet Relay Chat (IRC). Similarly, most other references to enterprisewide Internet strategy development focus on the specific technology aspect of Internet such as Navigating the Net, Mosaic, NetCruiser, SLIP/PPP connection, etc.

Technology focus is crucial, but now Internet is open to individuals and businesses in marketing, customer service, human resources, security and legal, as well as the technical experts within the Information Services division of an enterprise, as long as they abide by *Acceptable Use Policies* (AUP).

Chapter 4 of the book sets the guidelines for opportunity identification that will result in better Return On Investments (ROI). It addresses ROI by looking at what information costs and then formulating a mechanism to capture all the hard-to-measure items or "soft" items such as time saved, customer service, and management productivity improvements that the Internet delivers.

The extraordinary changes in the cost of processing, storing, and distributing information are transforming every aspect of the business world. The various enterprises can still articulate service levels, tasks, and performance indicators and calculate the hard costs of both building and maintaining the new base architecture. But if they look too closely at hard costs and benefits, they might miss valuable opportunities to reap intangible Internet and Intranet benefits. This is an excellent time to be learning about a whole new way of doing business. The challenge is to figure out some of the "soft" benefits that would come from switching to the Internet and the Intranet architectures. It observes that management productivity improves through the Internet and the Intranet, and it recommends a new measures: Return On Management (ROM).

The acceptable use policies are extremely important—businesses have severely damaged their reputations literally overnight, because they did not understand the Internet's rules and guidelines.

Chapter 5 focuses on issues such as who should be involved in putting together an enterprise's Internet policy and procedure, balancing the needs of the business with the Internet culture, and using the policy and procedure to educate the enterprise on how to work with the Internet and provide a positive presence for the enterprise. This chapter also takes a look at how to address the administrative "holes" that are present in the various organizations that pertain to use authorization, maintenance, and responsibility for WWW data and information integrity and security.

Chapter 6 uses case histories to further explain the process that some of the enterprises undertook in setting forth corporate oversight of the Internet, and acceptable use practices. No single policy or procedure can fit every type of enterprise, but the author hopes that the case histories will serve as a reference point to help those who undertake this same type of mission, and enlighten others within the Internet.

Chapter 7 summarizes the procedures outlined throughout the book. The four appendices are for those who, after reading the above parts, might have developed special interests in certain aspects of the Internet and the Intranet. Here we provide more technical definitions, special acronyms, and abbreviations commonly used in the Internet world, provide information on hardware and software requirements and sources, and classify Internet resources by their value to different enterprises and business functions.

Internet has doubled in size in the last six months, and will go through many more changes. Sites where resources are stored and ways of using the Internet and Intranet tools are in flux. If you can't find a particular resource where it is shown in the book, don't hesitate to use one of the search tools to relocate the information. Use this book as a get-up to the larger world, but be sure to maintain Hotlink to the Internet and Intranet servers and trade-up programs.

Chapter **1**

What Exactly Is the Internet?

Some of you may already be familiar with the Internet and know enough that you would like to skip over this section of the material and jump right onto the Internet strategy development. My advice to you is DON'T. Keep your enthusiasm, and watch it grow as you start at the beginning and build up excitement as you continue to learn more about this fascinating network connectivity we call the Internet.

BACKGROUND AND ORIGIN OF THE INTERNET

The Internet is basically a network of networks. The original network began about twenty-five years ago, in the late 1960s. It was created by a team of scientists from the Advanced Research Projects Agency (ARPA), a branch of the federal government's Department of Defense. It was called ARPANET and was intended to be used by the U.S. military as a vehicle for discussing research—a communications network that would be able to withstand any unforeseen events and give America the edge in any conflict. Soon the scientists realized that the network could be used for many other applications besides discussing research. As time progressed, more and more people learned about the benefits of electronic communications. They wanted to ask, answer, and listen to questions, and share the information and resources they had stored in their computers with other people. Thus, the need came about to serve more and more people who wanted to get on the ARPANET [1].

How ARPANET Became the Internet

It is vital to understand the history of the Internet in order to fully grasp what is happening today. We all know that the Internet is changing very rapidly, but it is a product of this history, with all the customs and layers of agreed upon rules and standards, called protocols, that were designed with the goals and objectives of the sponsors and inhabitants of the original networks in mind.

The protocols allowed dissimilar computer systems to communicate with each other, and routed data through multiple communications paths using groups of data or packets with their own destination addresses built in. These methods were so successful that civilian groups outside the U.S. government adopted these standards and created their own networks. Chief among these were Unix to Unix Copy Protocol (UUCP), and User Network (or USENET). The latter one started as a network for universities in the 1970s and further expanded into commercial services. Computer Sciences Network (CSNET) and "Because It's Time Network" (BITNET)—also a global academic and research network—evolved around 1981. These were much larger networks.

In the late 1980s, the National Science Foundation (NSF), another federal agency, brought networking technology and computers together. NSF created its own NSF Network (NSFNET) using the technology developed by ARPANET and its own very high-speed links, usually referred to as the Internet backbone. ARPANET itself formally expired in 1989. It is safe to say it was a victim of its own success.

Meanwhile, the NSFNET set the pace for further technical advancement. It linked newer, faster, shinier supercomputers with the aid of expanded, upgraded, and faster links. 1986, 1988, and 1990 marked the years when some of the specific upgrades took effect. Thus, what initially started as a 56 kbps network, primarily serving the National Science Foundation's six supercomputer centers, eventually began operating at 45 Mbps (T3). Figure 1.1 shows the Internet's backbone network as it was in 1993. The NSFNET backbone service ended in 1995 [2].

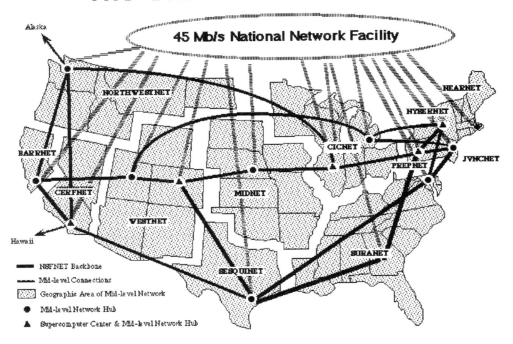

Source: U.S. National Science Foundation, 1996.

Figure 1.1 NSFNET Backbone Service 1993

The NSF expansion allowed campuses and research centers to use NSF's supercomputers, but the more interesting phenomenon was that the connections were increasingly used for both E-mail and transferring data and information files between sites. This growth and expansion of the network of networks came to be know as the Internet.

The Opportunity

In the course of time, a broader appreciation of the Internet and the groups that should have access to it has developed. The common metaphor for the Internet is the Information Superhighway. In more technical terms, the Internet is the world's largest open system: nobody "owns" the Internet, nor is there a central Internet hub. The network consists of thousands of servers and millions of clients.[2] Two protocols that form the basis for all Internet communications are Transmission Control Protocol and the Internet Protocol. These are commonly identified together as TCP/IP. For the day-to-day business operations, there are additional protocols. Subsequent paragraphs in this chapter will provide more details on those.

Another major facet of the Internet medium is that it is an emerging platform for mass media of a new type. It delivers personalized, individually aimed messages, and provides a collaborative work environment, covering wide areas and great distances.

Computer compatibility, as we discussed earlier, does not arise in the Internet environment. Instead, computers act as smart switches, connecting the various networks. They translate messages to and from computers using different communication protocols. In so doing, these computers can move packets of text, graphics, and audio information back and forth. Packets usually pass through several computers until the final destination is reached. Often when a pathway is blocked, the switches reroute the packet(s) automatically. At the final destinations, the packets get reassembled because they are usually too small to contain entire messages or graphics. Typically, a few seconds will elapse from the time the request is initiated to the time the whole packet is delivered.

Research scientists and college campuses around the world were the early users of the Internet, but its recent growth has been fueled by commercial subscribers, particularlysince the development of a HyperText-based,[3] technology—independent means of displaying

---

[2] A **server** is a computer and its software that stores, retrieves, and delivers data—"serving," or handling requests from clients. A **client** is a software application which enables you to access, view, and work with data provided by a server. This application runs on a PC or workstation.

[3] HyperText links allow easy navigation through material. They allow a reviewer to make a comment, pose a question, or clarify a point by creating additional links without disturbing the integrity of the original discussion.

textual, graphic, and audio information over the Internet. This means is commonly referred to as the World Wide Web (WWW) or simply the Web, and has created unlimited opportunities for communication. The Web will be defined more fully later in this chapter.

Businesses today use the Internet medium to post job openings and press releases and offer online product services and support, interactive product demonstrations, and video highlights or audio clips from recent presentations. The underlying concern is to enhance customer satisfaction and efficiency, and further increase productivity within the enterprises. The span of the Internet also allows tremendous opportunities for networking with other executives and staying abreast of new developments on any topic of interest. In the past, information was pushed at users; now it can be pulled [3].

How Internet Became Intranet

The possibilities being explored by enterprises are endless. By applying Internet technology for sharing information within their own corporate networks, enterprises have experimented with a special application that is being defined as "Intranet." Digital Equipment Corporation is one of the first companies to unleash the potential of Intranet. chapter 7 will present a case history about Digital's initial focus, later strategies to use Intranet to improve internal communications, and further efforts to modify its home-grown gateway software package, called the Screening External Access Link (SEAL) firewall, to provide security to businesses both inside and outside the enterprise. Sun Microsystems is another company that has been using Intranet quite extensively for the benefit of their employees. And with each passing day, enterprises such as Chevron, Goodyear, Levi Strauss, and Pfizer are beginning to use Intranet [4].

To all these enterprises, Intranet offers at the most basic level storage, search, and retrieval capabilities for static enterprise documents such as policy manuals and phone books. It also connects the different types of computers—PCs, Macs, or workstations—on the enterprise network. The underlying technology of Internet and Intranet and the Web makes it possible for any computer to display a document, no matter what kind of computer created it. Employees no longer need to be concerned about where the information is stored. A spreadsheet residing on a workstation in Hong Kong is as easy to retrieve as one in a particular employee's own desktop PC.

The Intranet at Morgan Stanley links thirty-seven offices around the world. Kevin Parker, the investment bank's chief information officer, says that the ability to distribute data and information seamlessly on a global basis is a problem Morgan Stanley has wrestled with for many years [5]. But now the Intranet provides information to all the thirty-seven offices in a way that is:

- Immediate

- Cost effective; Internal costs, according to related industry estimates, could be reduced by 20 percent over a period of two-four years [6]

- Easy to use

- Rich in format [4]

- Versatile

Morgan Stanley's example points out that the strengths that have made outwardly oriented Internet a popular tool for presenting marketing, advertising, and customer service information, are starting to help enterprises attend to internal business as well.

In a formal sense, the Internet is a wide-area network linking thousands of sites around the world. The communication, resource sharing, and navigation tools that were created especially for the Internet illustrate the extra-enterprise support technologies.

Communication tools are mainly electronic mail and discussion forums; resource sharing includes file transfer and remote terminal emulation, and navigation tools include the World Wide Web. At this stage, a few remarks about the Web will be helpful to better understand the migration of the Internet to the Intranet environment.

To the Internet users, the Web is a graphical front-end viewer that allows them to consult multimedia documents stored on servers around the world. The documents have hypertext links pointing to other documents on the same servers or on other servers. HyperText links are intrinsically appealing; they offer clean and intuitive access to the widest range of media types and make data access more successful. Also, because of its ability to strap on new technologies, programming languages, and media types such as audio and video, the Web integrates all other tools under a common umbrella. Many companies are leveraging the Web-based applications (e.g., publishing, database applications, distributed applications, etc.) to publish information to employees. This move has served as a catalyst for the Intranet phenomenon, causing the information systems inside the enterprise to look like the information systems outside the enterprise, and the internal and external information sources to commingle.

---

[4] This refers to a document formatting language developed by Microsoft for interchanging documents between Microsoft Word and other word processing packages.

The prospect of commingling internal and external systems raises various security and reliability concerns. It suggests that an organization must raise the awareness of the incidence of information gathering and use to a higher level of vigilance. Internet security is a dynamic and moving target. When dealing with electronic security in the 1990s, to paraphrase Reverend Dodson: "You have to run as hard as you can just to stay in the same place."[7]

To assimilate such security awareness in the Intranet environment, a few measures need to be enforced to ensure that intruders are not exploiting problems, and that users have not added a few holes to the network without informing the enterprise systems administrator. The underlying purpose here is to protect sensitive enterprise data residing on Intranet from the outside world. If anyone from outside wants access to the Intranet, there has to be authentication in place and verification processes that a requestor must pass through before being allowed in. The good news is that security packages are constantly being upgraded to provide better protection through encryption, authentication, and access control. These continual security enhancements are the reasons for growing commerce between Internet and Intranet. Many companies are opening parts of their internal networks to customers and suppliers who have Internet connections. A case in point is Federal Express. Customers can track their packages by logging onto FedEx's home page on the Internet, which is linked to the company's internal database [8].

APPLICATIONS AND TOOLS

Although an astronomical number of things can be done on the Internet and the Intranet, the most commonly known activities are:

> **Electronic Mail (E-mail)**—Sending and receiving electronic mail.

> **File Transfer Protocol (FTP)**—Transferring files between computers.

> **Telnet**—The word "Telnet" is both a command and a description of the service you receive when you use that command. It opens the door for you to login to computers around the world, whether you are a stranger to the second computer or not. [Hytelnet, a frequently updated database available for many computer systems, provides information about specific Telnet sites and aids in connecting to them.]

> **USENET (NetNews)**—Allows the user to participate in thousands of discussion groups that use newsreader software and servers.

The World Wide Web (WWW)—Refers to a system that brings world-wide Internet resources together into a seamless, interactive environment where information is easily found and retrieved.

Information Searches—Gopher, WAIS, Archie, Veronica, Finger, Net-find, etc., allow the user to search for specific information on the web.

Technical Aspects of Using

Electronic Mail

Electronic mail is commonly referred to as E-mail. It is an exchange of information and computer programs without incorporating postage. E-mail is very fast and very attractive to electronic customers! Messages are exchanged in minutes as opposed to days or even months using regular mail. With its varied uses today, your business can take advantage of E-mail to send information to potential clients and customers. Essentially, this involves connecting your enterprise's server to the Internet, which sends E-mail using the Simple Mail Transfer Program (SMTP). The E-mail information content could be an ongoing, specialized discussion of some sort,[5] a regular mailing, a text file, or even software [9].

E-mail derives its power from mailing lists and the software that generates them. A *mailing list* provides two things: (1) a list of mail recipients;[6] and (2) automatic distribution[7] of mail items to the hundreds or even thousands of "subscribers" on such a list. The convenience of mailing lists has produced many practical and economical business uses [10]. E-mail and mailing lists provide an opportunity for different enterprises to keep their customers updated about and interested in their products and services, and to respond to their ques-

---

[5] For instance, telephone conferences, while not uncommon in today's business environment, are slowly being replaced by E-Mail messages that are read and posted at convenient times and places. This reduces the considerable investment of time and effort in scheduling, planning, and discussion. E-Mail greatly facilitates group conferencing by enabling the members to participate at various times, from various locations.

[6] It is common for a mailing list to be centered around a specific topic such as commerce, science, academia, or entertainment.

[7] Listserv or Majordomo software handles these mailings by automatically placing subscription requests into a database and generating periodic mailings. The frequency of such mailings could be monthly, weekly, daily, or even hourly. These softwares run on certain specific platforms only. Consult your IS department to address the platform issues for your enterprises.

tions as quickly as possible. Mailing lists are very cost-effective—instead of enterprises seeking out customers, the customers come to them. Some specifics include:

Electronic Magazines or "E-Zines"

These are do-it-yourself publishing ventures that require little more than an E-mail account. Some enterprises may not need an entire magazine to market their businesses online, but the format is interesting and useful.

Group Discussions

Discussion lists are somewhat similar to the mailing lists. The major difference is that mailing lists are sent to subscribers in one batch, whereas discussion lists forward messages one at a time. Discussion lists can help businesses. For instance, IBM gains a solid marketing advantage merely by maintaining a forum that serves the needs of OS/2 users. A subscription to the OS/2 Users Mailing List provides ten to forty messages a day, all about OS/2. Subscribers respond to the person making the original inquiry or send response back to the full group. From IBM's standpoint, it really does not have to do a thing other than derive marketing benefits out of the E-mail traffic.

Frequently Asked Questions (FAQ)

Businesses often get asked some questions quite frequently. For those types of FAQ, there can be a prearranged set of answers. When customers send individual questions via E-mail, an administrative assistant can respond to a query instantly by using the Q & A format. This promotes good customer relations, as customers regard the enterprise as highly responsive.

No discussion on E-mail is complete without referring to its equalizing effect within a corporation. E-mail has created an openness within corporate environments that did not exist until recently. If we concentrate strictly on the business aspect of this phenomenon, reference could be made to some significant developments.

The most frequent business use of Internet connectivity involves internal and external communications: by using an E-mail package over the Internet, enterprises can establish contact with branches and work teams at many locations and can have high-speed access to vendors and customers. This is a virtual community in which people who might normally never meet or even communicate, find themselves in conversation about substantive matters [11].

NOTICE

Internet isn't the only system that uses E-Mail. Almost any computer network will allow you to exchange messages within the network.

More people today prefer communicating by E-mail rather than by phone or postal mail, because at all levels, from CEO to mailroom clerk, they feel freer to participate in discussions about the business. A person who sends a message by E-mail is more likely to receive a quick but thoughtful reply. Currently, the most commonly requested/required Internet service is E-mail. A note of caution should be given: E-mail is also one of the more abused services on the Internet and is the subject of genuine exchanges on industry-wide questions and improvement. Computer Emergency Response Team (CERT), a clearinghouse for Internet vulnerabilities at Carnegie Mellon University, advises that the main abuse of E-mail is to gain access to other services running on the same machine. There are state of the art technical solutions for E-mail security problems, but that is not the subject of this book. For those interested to learn more about these solutions, CERT Advisories would be the place to begin [12].

Network Newsgroups

File Transfer Protocol (FTP)

The method used to transfer files from one computer destination to another across the Internet is identified by the initials FTP. After E-mail, FTP creates the most traffic on the Internet [13]. The user can log into remote computers, search multiple directories, and retrieve and store files,[8] provided he or she has a valid ID and password with which to log on.

Thus, you can access a wealth of databases, programs, images, and other software resources (spreadsheet files, word processing files, graphics, etc.). Likewise, your enterprise can make its business available on the Internet. This entails setting up your enterprise's FTP server, enabling a portion of your system's directory structure to be open to the public. Your enterprise can set up the FTP server to allow only a few privileged users

---

[8] For enterprises that do not have IS departments, but find the idea of putting mailing lists to work in their businesses appealing, there is another solution. A service provider can, under contract, set up and maintain the list or simply provide server space if these enterprises have the in-house talent to maintain the list themselves.

to access your data via the Internet. The more popular configuration, however, is to allow "anonymous" FTP, where anyone entering their E-mail address as a password can enter the system. Under anonymous FTP, users have restrictions. They are allowed access to only part of the file system (typically in public areas[9]). An enterprise should treat FTP as a potentially powerful account that is best kept confined only to areas that cannot do damage to anything other than what is on the immediate server [14]. This sort of limitation enhances enterprise network security.[10]

Telnet

Simply speaking, Telnet is a TCP/IP that an operator uses to connect to a remote computer and run a program somewhere on the Internet as if he were sitting at a terminal linked directly to the remote computer. To accomplish this, enter the **Telnet** command with the remote computer address onto your own computer if you are already connected to the Internet or onto an Internet intermediary such as Delphi. Once the **Telnet** command is entered, the computer runs software that uses Telnet protocol to make the connection between the computers.

Like FTP, you can use Telnet in two ways—either to connect to a computer where you already have an account, or to login to a computer where you are a stranger. If you are wondering why you would want to use Telnet to gain access to a computer where you are already known, the answer is that Telnet can be a major convenience and save you money, especially if you happen to be sitting in a far off place, let us say Taiwan, and your account happens to be with a computer in Chicago.

Telnet is at its best when it allows you to access computers on which you have no account. There are some limitations that should be understood. Telnet is an invitation, and more often than not you will receive permission to use certain files within the remote computer. The type of programs for which you receive permission to use can vary—they could provide simple information like weather forecasts or complicated scientific data on the latest

---

[9] If an enterprise does not want users storing files on its system, they can change the permissions to read only, leaving the administrator with the sole ability to move files to the FTP directory.This refers to the contents of a directory named /pub, for which users have access to only a few commands for retrieving files and maneuvering within subdirectories.

[10] FTP is unique among the Internet services in that it requires permission for a remote host to open a local connection. In the event a user breaks out of the captive account, the intruder cannot do much damage because the enterprise server is dedicated to FTP and will not allow access to other machines within the enterprise network.

neural research. All in all, Telnet provides several services, each of which provides different forms of information.[11]

WARNING

There is a tremendous difference between being invited into a new computer through Telnet and cracking into someone else's private files through the use of an unauthorized user ID and password (a cracker is one who deliberately breaks into someone else's computer systems). With Telnet, you are asked to share other people's information in the spirit of mutual discovery. But if someone is cracking into a strange computer, that is breaking the law.

A note of caution about possible security breaches: login information may be captured through Telnet. To date, few network-specific attacks have taken place through Telnet; to be safe, an enterprise should allow Telnet connections only from approved outside hosts and with the tokens or plan for encryption that will be addressed later in this chapter under the section "Information Access: Security Concerns." [15]

USENET

There are several forms of discussion groups on the Internet covering a broad range of issues including technical, politics, and social topics. USENET is like a local bulletin board system where users regulate their own public discussions. The quality, accuracy, and usefulness of the information that the newsgroups generate vary widely, but there are a few newsgroups that are invaluable to network security administrators. These include sci.crypt, comp.security, alt.privacy, and comp.virus.[12] Altogether, there are over 17,000 newsgroups, including many that are not carried at all sites [16].

---

[11] Hytelnet allows you to locate Telnet resources around the Internet. There are two versions of Hytelnet: (1) a stand-alone version that could be easily downloaded and used on your own computer; and (2) an Internet service that is accessible through the Telnet.

The stand-alone version provides a large amount of information about Telnet sites and a copy is available through anonymous FTP. The Internet version enables you to choose the Telnet site that has the resources you need, and then you are connected to that site automatically. To gain access to the Internet version of Hytelnet, you need to use the WWW or Gopher location (defined later in this section).

[12] Newsgroups are built on a hierarchy. The first part of any name refers to the top-level hierarchy, such as "alt" (alternative), "biz" (business), "comp" (computer-related), "misc" (miscellaneous), and "rec" (recreational). Groups, names include one more qualifier to differentiate them from other subgroups under the same hierarchy.

USENET services are the favorites of the users, but the various alt.fan and alt.sex Newsgroups have been identified as indicative of the trivial nature of the Internet. The range of topics in such groups is a bit broad for some people's tastes, but two points should be underscored: (1) the "offending" newsgroups do not form the majority of overall Internet traffic and (2) an organization can limit the scope of USENET newsgroups to which its employees have access. chapters 6 and 8 cover more on this point.

The World Wide Web (WWW)

The Web provides access to a network of documents located around the world. It accomplishes this by using highlighted words that represent links to other documents. With clicks of a mouse, these links, referred to as the *HyperText Links*, make for easy navigation through material. They also allow a reviewer to make a comment, pose a question, or clarify a point by creating additional links without disturbing the integrity of the original discussion. For instance, a user may receive documents that let him/her select *Product Sales* from a list of choices. The server could then produce another page with pictorial descriptions of the products, along with pricing, an E-mail address for a sales contact, and the option to download a complete catalog [17].

A number of protocols will be used to carry out the various operations, as mentioned above. HyperText Transfer Protocol (HTTP) governs the delivery of HyperText along the Internet, and the HyperText Markup Language (HTML) codes create and format a Web document. Codes, called anchor codes, provide links within and between Web documents and to other Internet protocols. If the user selects a catalog from a particular business' Web page, FTP will be invoked to send the catalog. For other requests, similar protocols governing the respective facilities will come into play [18]. Today, a user, facilitated by a client software called a browser, can open documents on hundreds of specific subjects. This ease has transformed the Web into a highly interactive environment where text, graphics, and even sound and video can be supported [19]. Thus, HyperText is now a hypermedia environment which a user uses for any number of things:

- Information and research

- Business and commercial

- Personal communication and self-expression

- Entertainment and social interaction

The Web Browsers for Information Searching

A HyperText-based browser typically resides within a user's desk—top machine sometimes referred to as a client.

> **Mosaic**—The browser, which is in the public domain, is available free of charge from the National Center for Supercomputing Application's (NCSA) Internet server [20]. It relies on the TCP/IP communications protocols to retrieve files of information from server computers. If an enterprise allows Web requests to pass through their security firewall, Mosaic can retrieve data from computers located anywhere in the world. The retrieved file can be in text, video, or sound format. Businesses find such flexibility with format very appealing, as it breeds familiarity with the world of television and radio. Also, people often refer to Mosaic as the Web's "killer application," because early in its development cycle it made the Internet easy, powerful, and consistent across three desk top architectures, namely, PC, Macintosh, and workstations.

> **Netscape Navigator**—Marc Andreessen, creator of the NCSA Mosaic research prototype for the Internet says: "The real power comes with the creation and delivery of true interactive communications and applications." [21] Netscape's Navigator is the widely popular client software for enterprise networks and the Internet. It represents more than 85 percent usage on the World Wide Web, according to a variety of the Internet sites such as The Internet Financial Database, The Scripps Research Institute, TISC, and The University of Illinois at Urbana-Champaign [22]. The navigator provides a powerful environment for creating and maintaining live online applications for use within an enterprise or across the Internet. The applications include Web browsing and collaboration features such as interactive electronic mail, integrated threaded discussion groups, and support for interactive multimedia content.[13]

> **Netscape Navigator Gold**—This enhanced version of Netscape Navigator redefines the Internet client software standard by combining Web exploration E-mail, newsgroups, chat, and FTP capabilities with support for

---

[13] Embedded spreadsheets, animation, streaming audio and video, and 3-D capabilities that Live Objects provide.

additional new features [23]. Such new features facilitate new ways of communicating and conducting business within and beyond the enterprise.

The Leading Information Search-and-Query Tools

To make proper use of the Internet's millions of pieces of information, you will need help. Unless you use special tools and services, your search for any particular information can turn into a search for the proverbial needle in the haystack. The good news is that services are available through the Internet that can help you search or organize all the billion bits of information out there in the system [24]. Some of the *older* Internet search mechanisms search indices of databases for documents based on file titles, key words, or subject areas. Many servers still make good use of these tools:

> **Gopher**—This is a basic menu-based system, linking files on different computers throughout the Internet. It provides access to text documents, graphics, and digitized vocal annotations. The last item requires a separate computer application.

> **Wide Area Information System (WAIS)**—This allows the user to narrow searches by selecting a variety of sources. "Relevance feedback" is the embedded process that discards common words and ranks relevant documents according to the level or quality of the match, thereby improving the search.

> **Archie**—This is used for files accessible via anonymous FTP. Indices of files located at sites across the globe are generated by Archie servers and then the users receive appropriate Archie site name, IP address, and the location within the archive to retrieve the desired file.

> **Veronica**—This searches available Gopher sites for information on a specific topic.

> **WHOIS**—This was originally founded by the Defense Data Network's Network Information Center. Now it is run by InterNIC Registration Services in Herndon, VA. InterNIC has two unrestricted WHOIS services: a WHOIS database of users related to the networking structure and operation of the Internet; and a general WAIS database, containing global white page style listings of other users. WHOIS is accessed via Telnet, E-mail, Gopher, WAIS, and other WHOIS clients and tools.

> **Netfind**—According to statistics, this tool is very reliable. It is able to find five million+ users located within more than 9,000 domains [25].

Finger—This can be used if the user knows a person's domain address. All that the user has to do is type finger user@domain or finger @domain to see a list of users who are logged on. It is often exploited to find weaknesses in a private network. Accordingly, most commercial sites decline Finger requests.

A *newer* set of searching and indexing tools includes [26]:

WebCrawler—This provides a high-quality, fast, and free Internet search service available from America Online.

Yahoo!—This is a hierarchical subject-oriented guide for the World Wide Web and Internet. It lists sites, categorizing them under appropriate subjects.

Lycos—This is an excellent guide to the Internet, providing a catalog of URLs, a directory of the most popular sites, critical reviews of the Web's top sites, real-time news links, and so on.

InfoSeek—This is another free World Wide Web search service jointly offered by Infoseek, Netscape Communications, and Sun Microsystems Corporations. The service is accessed via Netscape's home page on the Internet. It is fast and accurate.

All of these services plus several others, make the WWW an easy environment to browse, even though it is the world's largest library of online information.

INFORMATION DISTRIBUTION

The NSFNET's high-speed, high-capacity lines, as discussed earlier, were known as the "Internet Backbone." In May 1993, a proposal received favorable consideration to upgrade NSFNET and strengthen interregional and national networking with a very high speed Backbone Network Service (vBNS), Network Access Points (NAPs), Routing Arbiter (RA), and *many* Network Service Providers (NSPs) [27]. Figure 1.2 depicts the new network architecture that is now a reality.

The vBNS links five NSF supercomputer centers and operates at minimum speeds of 155 Mbps. It offers a high-speed, high-bandwidth, virtual infrastructure for advanced applications. NAPs interconnect commercial Internet service providers. RA manages the ever-growing routing tables and databases for the service providers connecting at the NAPs.

The regional and midlevel networks pay commercial Internet service providers to get connected to NAPs.

Today, several hundred—maybe even thousand—regional networks connected to the Internet links sell Internet connections [28]. These have become fast growing businesses that offer different Internet access options.

Connectivity Providers

Access to the Internet can be provided by any local, regional, or national service provider, at whatever rates they set. Some services may be expensive, and some may require software that runs only on PCs and Macintosh. According to a recent NBC report [29], "connecting people in new ways has become a major business in this country."

Accessing the Internet

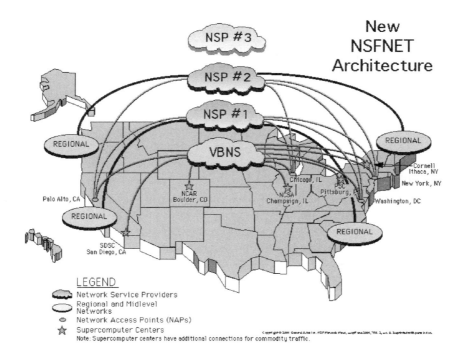

Source: U.S. National Science Foundation, 1996.

Figure 1.2 The New NSFNET Connections

In attempting to evaluate these service providers, different enterprises must identify the qualifications important to the organization, Table 1.1 identifies the various types of Internet service providers and their characteristics.

NOTICE

To immediately clear up any misconceptions, it is not your personal computer that will be connected to the Internet. Rather, your PC will be the device that allows you to dial into a local Internet system.

Service providers offer access to the Internet in one of the four ways described below. It is not the intent of this section to cover all the technical details of each level of service, or the type of service offered by every Internet service provider. Such technical details on

Type of Internet Service Provider	Examples	Characteristics
Interexchange Carriers (IXCs), Value-added Networks	Sprint, MCI Communications, Advantis, AT&T	Ubiquitous service, full-time help desks. Provider manages and maintains network, including hardware and leased lines. Highest level of quality customer support.
Large Commercial Internet Providers (CIPs)	Advanced Network & Services, Inc. (ANS); Performance Systems International, Inc. (PSI); UUNet Technologies, Inc. (Alternet)	Coverage is throughout U.S. Access is through leased lines from 56 Kbps to 1.544 Mbps, frame relay, ISDN, coaxial cable in selected location, async dial-up. Provider will manage equipment, configure domain name server, E-mail gateway, FTP server, furnish space on its own FTP servers, and provide consulting services.

Table 1.1 The Five Types of Internet Service Providers

Type of Internet Service Provider	Examples	Characteristics
Regional Providers	The Pipeline, Merit Network, Inc., PREPNet, Real-Time Communications, Texas MetroNet, Teleport, SSNet, Inc.	Often spin-offs of academic providers, generally inexperienced staff, uncertain customer support.
Online Services	America Online (AOL), Delphi, Prodigy, CompuServe,Genie, ImagiNation, ZiffNet	Offer a variety of features and services, such as news, weather, sports, shopping, travel arrangements, bulletin boards (also called forums or round-tables) on many interests, games, online chatting, investment advice and services, educational services, reference works and more. Some of these deliver integrated Internet business solutions.
Bulletin Board Systems	35,000+ in North America	Typically local dial-in; may have "door" to the Internet.

Source: This draws on several sources. Chief among them are Phillips Publishing Inc.'s *Access Wars Brewing, PIT ISPs Against Telcos—MCI and PSINet Executives Discuss the Future of the Access Market*, Press Release, 9 September 1995; Southern Electronic Pushing's *Internet Providers Face Formidable Competitors; Phone Companies Well Poised to Offer Net Access*, HeadsUp, 30 September 1995; Johna Till Johnson's *The Internet: Corporations Worldwide Make the Connection, Data Communications*, April 1994, and The Gartner Group's *ECS Strategy Analysis Report,* December 21, 1994.

Table 1.1 The Five Types of Internet Service Providers (continued)

exactly how to connect with the Internet are given in Appendix C. Appendix D provides-the list of the service providers.[14]

---

[14] The list is changing every day, and literally hundreds of local, regional national, and international vendors will be added to this list by the time this book goes to print. So what we have in Appendix D is the list of the most popular current national and regional Internet service providers that provide links to the Internet.

Remote Network Access or Gateway or Online Services

America Online, Delphi, CompuServe, GEnie, MCI Mail, and some commercial Bulletin Board Services (BBS) such as FidoNet, are examples of Gateway Services. They provide limited Internet access. This type of access is not really for business users, because most commercial providers, as well as the BBS, are simply gateways to the Internet E-Mail. They are not on the Internet. Consequently, there are significant delays in mail delivery, size limitations on E-mail messages, and limitations on real Internet access. This last problem may change in the near future.

Dial-Up or Shell Accounts

This is the simplest and least expensive way of accessing the Internet. Equipment needs are very modest for this kind of connectivity. This option takes care of most of the needs of small to medium-sized enterprises that are not computer intensive. This is equally good for some functions of larger businesses.

Often, this type of connection is referred to as indirect, because the dial-up connection is handled through another computer that is a part of the Internet. The process begins with a user dialing a phone number for a "remote" computer (meaning that it's a machine other than the user's own, not because it's far away. It might be in the same room as the user's computer and it would still be remote). After answering a few questions, the user is connected to the computer's Internet connection to obtain the information desired. Users are typically billed on a per-hour basis, although some Internet providers offer flat-rate service. The advantages are low-cost for users and minimal hardware and software requirements. A drawback is that some services using graphical interfaces aren't available to dial-up sessions.

Serial Line Internet Protocol (SLIP)

This is a dial-up direct connection service that uses normal phone lines, modems, and special software package conforming to SLIP standards. This mode of connection is superior to dial-up because: (1) SLIP can be attached to an enterprise's local area network (LAN), allowing for multiple users; (2) the user's system is actually connected to the Internet as a node, so they can avail themselves of all Internet services; (3) users do not have to concern themselves with the details and protocols of working with a remote host; and (4) access tools run on the user's system rather than on a remote host.

The telephone charges are modest, requiring only a normal phone line. The up-front equipment costs are a bit higher than for simple dial-up, requiring a 486 PC or a Macintosh

Quadra. In this particular set up, the service provider is acting only as an intermediate connection point, so the users must have a computer with independent storage and sufficient performance to host necessary software, and a high-speed modem—9,600 baud minimum, 14,400 or 28,000 recommended. Users are generally billed on a per-hour basis, although some Internet providers offer flat-rate service.

Point to Point Protocol (PPP)

This is the functional replacement for SLIP. The Internet standard Point to Point Protocol (PPP) corrects many of the deficiencies in SLIP. For instance, PPP is faster and more stable, prompting many network providers to offer PPP as the sole access protocol for a cost effective mechanism for corporate Internet connections.

Dedicated Leased Lines and Registering as an Internet Node

Many businesses are interested in having their company names as a node name, such as **Satlink.com**. There are two ways to become a true node: (1) through a full dedicated line connection; and (2) through certain full-time SLIP connections. However, many dial-up service providers allow companies to have domain names[15] through the use of alias, which allows a company to appear as though it is Satlink.com without actually being a node.

CONNECTION	SPEED	FEATURES
Gateways Dial-up	0-28.8 Kbps	Temporarily placed on the Internet.
SLIP PPP	0-28.8 Kbps	Employ local software on the user's own computer, allowing for fancy Graphical User Interfaces that make the Internet easier to use for novices.
Leased line	56 Kbps to 768 Kbps	Most direct connection to the Internet—server is actually on the Internet.

Table 1.2 Internet Connections and Phone Line Types

The domain names are assigned on a first-come, first-served basis. To start a new Internet node, an enterprise must first contact the Internetworking Information Center (InterNIC) of Network Solutions, Inc. of Herndon, VA for a domain name, as well as fees a. pertinent information. Once the domain name is registered, the enterprise will be use it. There could be several weeks delay in the processing time.

INFORMATION ACCESS: SECURITY CONCERNS

The Internet, as a public network, provides instant global, access to information resources but unauthorized computer users, called "crackers" or "hackers" are always a major source of concern. They consider it a great sport to try to skirt any security measure; accordingly, they often fraudulently access Internet accessible networked systems. As the Internet continues to evolve into a commerce environment, security for network components and services must be offered. There are, indeed, tools available to protect information and systems against compromise, intrusion, or misuse.

Firewalls

Firewalls filter the packets that are generated by the Internet's baseline protocol, TCP/IP, which was not built for security. Usually offered as turnkey hardware/software packages, these firewalls could be configured to *allow* access only from specific hosts and networks, or an enterprise could set up its firewalls to *prevent* access from specific hosts. There could also be different levels of access to various hosts. For instance, a preferred host may have full access, whereas another host may be permitted to access only certain portions of an enterprise host's directory structure, as discussed under anonymous FTP [30].

Assured Pipelines

To obtain a higher level of security, an enterprise can spend more to install more sophis-

---

15 Domain names are Internet "addresses." Internetworking Information Center (InterNIC) of Network Solutions Inc. assigns and keeps track of all domain names in the United States. Under contract with NSF since April 1993, it administers a registration process that includes the creation of a database which maps the names to the numbers used for Internet routing.

As interest in the Internet rose beyond expectation, the demand for domain names had gone beyond NSF's ability to continue to fund the service. Back in the spring of 1993, new domain names were registered at the rate of 400 per month. By October 1994, there were about 2,000 registrations per month, and this figure went beyond 20,000 per month by the end of 1995. Less than 3 percent of domain names are higher educational (.edu) or government (.gov)—most are commercial users (.com).

In view of the growing demand, NSF privatized the commercial aspects of the ever-growing Internet. NSF's funding for domain name services expired October 1, 1995, and now commercial, network, and not-for-profit registrants pay a $100 fee to register a name for two years, followed by $50 annual fees beyond the first two years. Prior to this, the Internet's domain registration process had been funded by the tax payers.

ticated methods of preventing access. For instance, an assured pipeline looks at an entire request for data and then determines the validity of the request. Requests that are inappropriate can be rerouted away from the Internet and those files that contain, for instance, the word confidential, can never be sent over the Internet, regardless of where the request originates—at the system administrator level or any other user level. The minimum price tag for such an enhanced security system could be $30,000; however, the important point is that these can be set up to enforce specific security policies that an enterprise desires [31].

Cryptographic Protection

As information transits the Internet, encryption can prevent interception by eavesdroppers. For instance:

> If Internet is used for exchanging information among branch offices of an enterprise, hardware encryption devices available at a reasonable cost can secure all traffic between these offices.

> Software packages can also provide encryption and decryption for message security. Software encryption is typically used in conjunction with specific applications.

E-mail Encryption

Sensitive E-mail can be protected either by encrypting the mail itself or the files attached to it. An enterprise can use Phil Zimmermann's Pretty Good Privacy (PGP), which is the most famous encryption tool on the Internet [32]. PGP combines public and secret keys from two users to encrypt a file or part of a mail message; one must have the public key of the recipient of an encrypted file in order to be able to decrypt the file [33]. MIT Kerberos' authentication scheme is an alternative that can be used to secure specific messages or to protect a server's protocol level [34].

CONCLUSION

It is important to evaluate the tools and procedures mentioned above to protect an enterprise's information assets. For individual Internet connections used for normal business purposes, security is not often a problem. The same holds true about those Web servers which are separate from the internal networks and are intended for public access. The point to underscore here is that an enterprise should *not* overreact and incur *unnecessary* expenses. Rather, it should have a corporate Internet security strategy and security policies and procedures should form an integral part of it. chapter 7 provides guidelines for such considerations, but those should not be construed as a complete resource guide for implementing security precautions. An enterprise's Internet usage can be as secure as required, and that means, above and beyond everything that has been delineated in chapter 7, an enterprise must promulgate, if the environment so warrants, more detailed security checklist to:

- Identify enterprise systems

- Classify internal systems

- Identify gateway machines

- Secure gateway systems

- Develop a comprehensive Firewall model

- Scan systems for external vulnerabilities/exposure

- Perform vulnerability assessment on internal systems

- Correct identified exposures from external scans

- Correct identified exposures from internal scans

- Establish password checks

- Enforce password exchange cycle

- Make use of onetime password technologies

- Make use of encryption

- Make use of file access policies

- Be proactive

- Subscribe to mailing lists such as *majordomo@greatcircle.com, cert-advisry-request@cert.org, etc.*

- Subscribe to security newsgroups such as *comp.security.unix, alt.security, comp.security.announce, alt.security.pgp, alt.security.keydist, alt.security.ripem, comp.protocols.kerberos, comp.virus, comp.risks, etc.*

- Develop notification mailing lists

Chapter **2**

What Functions Are Driving an Enterprise's Adoption of the Internet?

"It connects us to the world," says Lee Penn of DLP Technologies in Anderson Township. "There is a lot of information on Internet that people want access to And if you are commercially attached to Internet, you can do business. There is a local consortium of five diverse companies—I can't tell you who—that want to have access to each other's inventory. They want an easy way to cross-check what's on hand, and Internet helps with that. That's one way it's applicable to business." Penn talks to others, exchanging ideas that move their common knowledge forward.

Source: "Endless Possibilities on User-friendly Internet," *Internet Millions!* M.O.R.E. Inc., 1995, p.2

APPROACHING THE INTERNET AS A STRATEGIC BUSINESS TOOL

Many organizations are investigating the use of the Internet for commercial applications because the transaction cost of the network is low and the reach is wide. Large, medium, and small enterprises exchange large technical data files, transmit orders and specifications to trading partners, and give potential customers access to electronic catalogs. In March of 1995, CIO magazine conducted a survey of more than 200 Information Services and senior executives to learn how involved their organizations are in the Internet.

The conclusions drawn from the survey showed that nearly 75 percent were active on the Internet, using FTP, E-Mail, Gopher, and other Internet services. But 6 percent of the respondents were unaware if their enterprises were active on the Net (See Figure 2.1).

PERCENTAGE OF RESPONDENTS

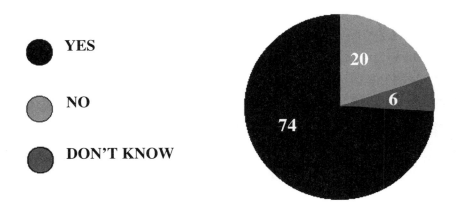

Source: CIO magazine conducted survey, http://www.cio.com/WebMaster/webciosurv.html

Figure 2.1 Enterprise's Use of the Internet Services: FTP, E-Mail, Gopher, etc.

Those respondents who were active noted that their current activities are not serious enough, but will become so within a year's time. Further, they pointed out that the focus will most likely shift toward external projects (See Figure 2.2).

In virtually every industry, competition has reached a new level of intensity. Mere survival warrants that an enterprise perform at unprecedented levels of effectiveness. The pressures include, but are not limited to, several factors:

> **Marketplace Environment**—Mass marketing today needs to be fine tuned by reaching the right segments with the right messages.

> **Structural Changes**—New business practices are emerging whereby organizations and people must work together, giving rise to virtual corporations, collaborative product development, and integrated supply chain management.

> **Demand for Quality and Customer Service**—Businesses are expected to provide prompt and individualized support to customers.

PERCENTAGE OF RESPONSES

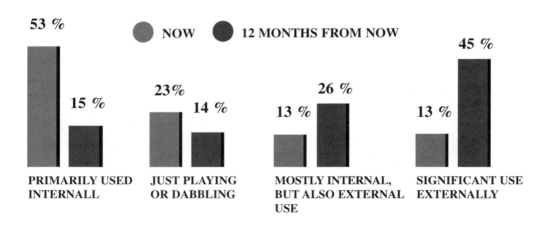

Source: CIO magazine conducted survey results at http://www.cio.com/WebMaster/webciosurv.html

Figure 2.2 Various Enterprises' Web-related Activities

In view of these requirements for specific business-oriented capabilities, it is not surprising that marketing, end users, management, lines of business, and business strategy groups are all requesting Internet activities. Figure 2.3 identifies the departments that are driving the Web adoption programs. In most enterprises, Information Technology (IT) and communications/public relations divisions remain at the center of Internet programs, running the Fortune 1,000 Web sites that the Forrester Research Group found when they interviewed fifty-one companies about the Internet [1]. But IT and communications/public relations also work alongside other groups. The Forrester Report identifies several companies that attest to this new thrust from within the companies. For instance, it refers to an industrial equipment company, saying, "The concept of putting out applications on the Internet is now being pushed by the more advanced business groups. They feel there is a lot of competitive pressure and don't feel they can afford not to go forward."

TOP SIX DEPARTMENTS THAT ARE DRIVING WEB ADOPTION

PERCENT OF RESPONDENTS
(MUTIPLE RESPONSES ALLOWED)

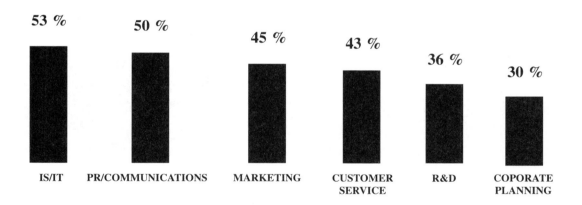

OTHER DEPARTMENTS: HUMAN RESOURCES (14%), PURCHING (12), LEAGL (4%)

Source: Corporate Web survey at http://www.cio.com/WebMaster/webciosurv.htmlsurv.html

Figure 2.3 Top Six Departments that Are Driving Web Adoption

The CIO Survey also queried the 18 percent with no plans to join (see Figure 2.4) as to why they were holding out. Their answers included "Unfamiliar with Web" to simply "I don't know." For those people familiar with the Internet, it is a new business tool which enables communications, especially interenterprise communications, to be used as a strategic competitive weapon. UUNet Home Page (http://www.uu.net/busguide.html) identifies a plethora of applications from marketing to customer support to collaborative development of electronic commerce. Many other applications are yet to be discovered; the question is, if the benefits exist, how should an enterprise proceed with the Internet? The Forrester Report makes the following recommendations to the CIO community:

- Don't react—anticipate.

- Invest in Internet technology.

- Provide infrastructure and vision—don't try to control.

PERCENTAGE OF RESPONDENTS

 **ALREADY HAVE A PRESENCE**

 **PLAN TO HAVE A PRESENCE**

HAVE NO PLANS

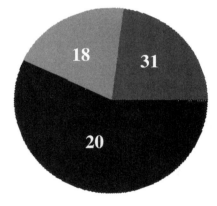

Source: http://www.cio.com/WebMaster/webciosurv.html

Figure 2.4 Corporate Web Use Survey

This book promises to offer practical techniques for determining where to invest and how much to invest. Before identifying and discussing the techniques for analysis of Internet investments that add value to enterprises' strategy, quality, and security [2], CEOs, CFOs, and CIOs need to fully address their organizations' business concerns and the functional requirements of the enterprises.

FUNCTIONAL REQUIREMENTS: THE BROADER ISSUES

As you prepare your guidelines and policies to accelerate the development of the enterprise Internet, bear in mind that there is no inevitable force pulling the advanced applications of the Internet into being, nor are the desirable future characteristics of the Internet enough to make it happen.

REVIEW

"Speed at which bits may race to their destination to be reassembled into words or images is not enough to judge the Internet. The important factor is how well these technical capabilities make the enterprise and its employees fast, efficient, and more responsive to their customer [3]." John Coviello, vice president of Sabre Computer Services, said it best: "the most important performance measurements for the Internet are not merely technical, but include social dimensions." [Personal conversation with the author.]

Success in each enterprise requires the articulation of the range of activities which are available not only by the fact that the Internet exists, but also by the way it can enable "virtual alliances" with other trading partners. Functional requirements that drive the Internet usage strategy for the large, medium, and small enterprises need to be clearly identified, as well as opportunities for various enterprises' intermediate goals and objectives and their successful negotiation of outcomes involving a multitude of different parties. Imagine a future that is already taking shape where:

- Companies form alliances rapidly and easily to produce new products and employ advanced manufacturing concepts.

- "Software system brokers" connect users with a need for temporary access to sophisticated manufacturing tools that would normally be too expensive to acquire.

- Manufacturers and suppliers use "intelligent" procurement systems to facilitate and accelerate parts procurement, billing, and payment transactions, thereby reducing costs, improving accuracy, and meeting customer demand in a timely manner.

Today, the increased pressure to reduce innovation time, the growing technical complexity of products and processes, and the need to be responsive to external demand for quality, customization, and cost are rapidly altering the functional requirements. This is true for large, medium, and small enterprises alike.

How are the various enterprises seeking ways to redefine the functional interface requirements or break down the walls that have traditionally separated operations within an enterprise as well as the barriers that have inhibited communication with customers, suppliers, partners, and even competitors? Some of the discussions are presented as questions. As you read the examples, your input in helping to answer these questions and to raise other relevant issues will guide your enterprise's policies and investments to accelerate the Internet connectivity.

Manufacturing and the Internet

For the purpose of this discussion, "manufacturing" refers to the discrete parts manufacturing industry. It encompasses everything from automobile and computer products to wood furniture. Today's manufacturers face intense competition that threatens their very survival. One of their basic functional requirements to stay competitive is to improve productivity.

Many recent studies indicate that the design process exerts the most influence over a product's life cycle: approximately 60 percent of a product's cost is fixed early in the process of design. An Institute for Defense Analysis report noted that advanced manufacturing techniques that enable the rapid exchange of information not only increase quality and cut the number of design changes by 50 percent, but also reduce total costs by 30-60 percent and development time by 35-60 percent, design and product defects by 30-80 percent, and scrap work by 58-75 percent [5].

Intel Corporation used computer-based concurrent engineering and improved communication among design teams to provide simulation, consistency, and the sharing of data among concurrent work teams. This process improvement reduced the time from design-to-sample by half, even though product complexity doubled. The company also achieved a 95 percent success rate on the first silicon fabrication of new products. These successes enabled Intel Corporation to retain 95 percent of the flash memory market even in the face of a strong Japanese competition [6].

Implementation of proprietary concurrent engineering systems has allowed Japanese auto makers to decrease time-to-market for new cars by more than 30 percent, enabling them to gain considerable market share and to increase pressure on U.S. auto makers [7].

Another study, *CALS Contractor Integrated Technical Information Service* (CITIS): *Business Case Feasibility Study*, evaluated the impact of a common data management, storage, retrieval, and exchange service for transferring in a standard digital format all contractor design and manufacturing data among the Air Force and its B2 subcontractors. The savings indicated 50 percent reduction in the number of attendees at meetings between contractors and the Air Force, a 5.4 percent reduction in the total B2 spare dollars, a 23 percent reduction in modification lead time, a 1.8 percent increase in the average availability of aircraft fleet, and a 90 percent reduction in the contractor data submittals. Estimated total cost savings ranged from a minimum of $536 million to a maximum of $894 million, for investments that ranged from $9 million to $30 million [8].

Harley Davidson used just-in-time inventory control and total quality management practice to reduce manufacturing cycle time for motorcycle frames from seventy-two days to two. The company also improved final product quality from 50 percent to 99 percent.

By using the same productivity improvement programs, Digital Equipment Corporation reduced overall inventory from sixteen weeks to three, and its defect rate went down from 17 percent to 3 percent; 3M also experienced a seventy-fold reduction in critical defects, appearance defects, and packaging problems [9].

The French automobile manufacturer PSA Peugeot Citron also had success in creating closer, more efficient ties with its many suppliers and implementing "just-in-time," "quick response" inventory control. They used an electronic communications network, ODETTE (Organization of Data Exchange via TeleTransmission in Europe). It improved inventory turnover by nearly 40 percent, reduced the number of unassembled cars on the line by 70 percent, and provided customers with nearly 30 percent more models to choose from. The company increased the quality of its products and customer satisfaction levels, as evidenced by its departure from a monthly order cycle to a multi-day one [10].

These trends indicate that manufacturers, irrespective of their sizes, are developing and implementing automated technologies, such as computer-aided-design (CAD), computer-aided manufacturing (CAM), computer-aided engineering (CAE), and computer-integrated manufacturing (CIM) to increase the speed of design and production and to reduce costs. Although these automations have so far been accomplished with a high degree of sophistication, their focus remains narrow.

To remain competitive, many large enterprises, such as Boeing, General Motors, Ford, Newport News Shipbuilding, Caterpillar, and Intel are instituting more programs to address one of the other key functional requirements: *networking capabilities*. They view Manufacturing Extension Partnership (MEP) as a very important step toward global competitiveness. MEP electronically connects a vast array of technology resources available throughout the nation. These resources provide technical assistance with new management and organizational practices, shop floor design, manufacturing process evaluation, workflow education, training programs, and deployment of appropriate advanced manufacturing technologies and manufacturing best practices. To these resources, the larger enterprises are adding services requested by clients. They are implementing user friendly frontend for transparent access to data repositories resident on the major network systems (e.g., WWW, Gopher, WAIS, etc.). Their future programs also include additions of databases of best practices, enterprise information, video teleconferencing, online training, product data, and electronic commerce capability to the system.

REVIEW

Are you capable of transmitting data quickly and efficiently from one application to another inside and outside your enterprise's operation?

Can you afford to remain isolated and incapable of integrating your applications interaction with other companies, suppliers, and customers in a timely and cost effective manner?

Or, do you need to be connected to a set of online services, including directories, design and analysis tools, databases, and search mechanisms for the secure, easy, and timely exchange of manufacturing information in such areas as process analysis, benchmarking, quality assessment, and best practices, as well as to a potential user base of 370,000 other small- and medium-sized manufacturers?

So, the question to ask is what form of industrial extension services, enterprise integration, and/or electronic commerce is best suited for your enterprise?

Under the auspices of Smart Valley, Inc., a consortium, which includes Hewlett Packard, Intel, Sun Microsystems, Apple, National Semiconductor, and Texas Instruments, was created. It is called *CommerceNet*. It is an open, Internet-based infrastructure to revolutionalize the way companies design, manufacture, sell, and support their products. It makes interactions with customers, suppliers, and partners efficient, high quality, flexible, and responsive.

The Forrester Report makes reference to the fact that the focus and passion of the network industry has turned toward the Internet for a sustained period—years, not months. You are a decision maker and even though some of you may have decided just to wait and see, do you need to develop the means to:

- Better understand your own and other's information requirements and flows?

- Reduce the time it takes for your enterprise to design and manufacture products and get them to market?

- Enhance and adopt key technologies to enable advanced, highly integrated systems to "plug in" a variety of focused engineering tools, thereby ensuring your enterprise of the use of numerous suppliers, as well as additional next generation tools?

We have raised these ideas as questions because it is imperative that you think strategically about your investments in infrastructure technologies, tools, and services, and make all investments in the context of a long-term business strategy that places emphasis on information management and its use in future economic competitiveness. Demonstration and testing of enterprise integration will help you see the benefits of seamless exchange and use of information throughout your enterprise. This will also provide a model for your manufacturing division to build toward, encourage your enterprise planners to plan investments in terms of a long-term business strategy, and avoid "islands of automation" or stove-pipe situations.

The importance of strategic thinking needs to be underscored by the fact that large, medium, and small enterprises alike are inhibited by the difficulties of identifying and assessing technology trends, developing adequate investment decision making and strategic planning models, implementing new technologies and migrating from old (legacy) systems, and, above all, tying all these factors together by presenting a comprehensive business case. Besides, there is the perceived threat of advanced manufacturing applications on traditional ways of performing work. This stems from inexperience with newer information technologies. User acceptance and comfort and familiarity with Internet networking technology and its opportunities for improving competitiveness and economic performance can be assured only if and when you and your enterprise address your networking capabilities and the overall functional requirements in terms of the following manufacturing functions:

- transmission, translation, exchange, and down-loading of electronic design Initial Graphic Exchange Specification, and business transaction data Electronic Data Interchange;

- electronic bidding and proposal, billing, and payment processes;

- conversion and translation of data, including legacy (Computer-aided) data;

- automation of engineering and design change; and

- search, identification, location, communication, and coordination of suppliers, customers, partners, and others.

Health Care and the Internet

The health sector is far behind the banks, airlines, stock markets, and even salvage yards in applying information and communication technologies. Most hospitals and clinics use computers for billing purposes, and for patient admission, discharge, and transfer functions, but not nearly as much for clinical purposes. Consequently, patient-care information is not widely shared, even though in recent years some hospitals and clinics have linked caregivers together over local- or wide-area networks. Generally, it is impossible to examine aggregate data across a large number of similar patients, or to study a case history by tracing longitudinally the course of an individual patient with appropriate documentation of the decisions, consultations, and sequence of interventions that were made to attend to that particular patient's needs. So, the basic functional need always exists:

> a) to increase knowledge about the medical effectiveness of alternative treatments; and

> b) to make it available to providers and consumers of health care.

SCENARIO

A state public health official is looking at a statistically significant high incidence of children treated for respiratory disorders in a community. She retrieves state's health records from a statewide information network resident on the Internet. After querying the immunization records, she finds out that some children, who were not vaccinated, have been diagnosed with whooping cough (pertussis). A call to the community's health department further verifies that the data is accurate. Her next query to the information system reveals that there is a shortage of pertussis vaccine in that community. She takes an Action Item to immediately call the four neighboring communities with ample supplies and requests them to ship half of their vaccine to the affected community. She then advises the affected community about the actions she has taken and also brings herself up-to-date on their plans to cure the situation. After all is said and done, she returns to her examination of the state's health profile and customers in timely and cost effective manner.

Automated, uniformly defined, linked, and anonymously aggregated data on patient treatment and outcomes are increasing in demand throughout the healthcare industry. They are much sought after for various reasons, including clinical purposes, quality assurance, utilization review, business planning, administration, and public health. For instance, Physician Data Query (PDQ), a National Cancer Institute cancer treatment information system, is increasingly being used by panels of clinical cancer experts because it contains the most up-to-date information regarding the cancer treatments and research findings worldwide. The literature on cancer prevention and treatment trials are synthesized monthly and updated continually using *CancerFax* and *CancerNet*. This is the information about state of the art therapy and clinical treatment that the physicians look for in order to gain an insight into each cancer and its stages and then to advise their patients accordingly.

Based on the above discussion, we want to make two observations. The first, which underlies and shapes the second, is that in spite of all the progress in information technology, health care providers do not yet enjoy the means to keep abreast of the information generated in their fields of specialty. More often than not they simply fail to marshall all relevant information on a patient when making medical decisions. Additionally, there are problems of merging administrative and clinical information to make rational decisions concerning health institutions, quality of care, service availability, pricing, and so forth.

REVIEW

Is it your enterprise's goal to generate the knowledge about treatments and technologies that work best for specific clinical conditions?

Can Internet networking facilitate your healthcare enterprise by disseminating data based on the Net, adding value through the evaluation of the information gained from the data on the Net, and converting that information into useful knowledge?

There are substantial geographical variations in medical practices, as well as unexplained differences in decisions about the best treatment for similar patients with the same conditions. An Automated Antibiotic Consultant software program, introduced into its Health Evaluation through Logical Processing (HELP) system by Latter Day Saints Hospital in Salt Lake City, proved to be able to support physicians' decisions under conditions of uncertainty whether accessed on site or through a medical network. The Automated Consultant advised on appropriate antibiotics 94 percent of the time [11]. The HELP system was also able to determine the optimal timing (zero to two hours) of antibiotics before surgery to reduce the risk of post-surgical infection [12].

REVIEW

The HELP system produced good, uniform data. The question before us is whether it is advantageous to obtain accurate patient care data. The Workgroup for Electronic Data Interchange (WEDI) evaluated the costs and benefits of implementing electronic data interchange for administrative healthcare activities. It argued that the cumulative net savings over the remainder of this decade would amount to over $42 billion [13].

Where Do You Want to Be?

Kaiser Permanente in California and Mayo Foundation in Minnesota have efforts underway to build computer-based patient records and to export common definitions and reporting systems to all their sites nationwide. Washington, Iowa, Vermont, New York, Minnesota, and Ohio, as well as the city of Memphis received a grant from John A. Hartford Foundation to initiate projects on Community Health Management Information System. Their aim is to extract patient, provider, and service data from claims and encounters, and then store them in a shared community data repository. Subject to further enhancements, this could include condition-specific data and patient-centered surveys.

Several other health information networks are in planning stages, without a common model to guide them. The potential for your enterprise to link national and community networks with homes, offices, and health institutions by means of the Internet is something for you to evaluate and demonstrate. If you don't know about your healthcare enterprise's activity on the Net, ask yourself and your colleagues the following review questions:

REVIEW

Does your healthcare enterprise need to share patient care data across different computer information systems?

Does it need access to health data repositories that are located regionally across the United States, or distributed among local communities, or that may all be in one central location, safeguarding the confidentiality of patient-identifiable data?

Does your enterprise actively promote efficient use of medical services and administrative electronic data systems to improve the efficiency of medical claims handling and payment?

Does your enterprise need to transmit medical and patient images, consumer health information and decision analysis, and video consultations with physicians, specialists, and patients with similar conditions across geographic distances?

Your answers to these questions should reveal whether or not you have the basic functional requirement to install the Internet connectivity in your enterprise, and if so, where the most beneficial applications are likely to be!

Transportation Enterprise and the Internet

Transportation represents a massive enterprise with its system infrastructure valued at $2.4 trillion. There are over 2,000 commercial airports, seaports, and intermodal terminals; 305,767 km of petroleum pipelines; more than 402,325 km of rail and rapid transit lines; highways and roads, used by some 200 million cars, trucks, and buses, as well as navigable waterways used by 35,000 commercial vessels, ferries, and barges. A 1994 report by the U.S. Department of Transportation highlights that the number of civil aircraft alone using the infrastructure is over 300,000. [Refer to the Department of Transportation Strategic Plan, U.S. Department of Transportation, January 1994].

Could the emerging Internet provide new ways for operators to improve transportation system performance, thereby enabling travelers and shippers to make informed choices? The author is familiar with the aviation information and communication technology areas; the issues and concerns in this section, therefore, address chiefly aviation information systems and improvements that could make these systems truly responsive to today's customer preferences and needs. There is, of course, a dual purpose here. We will use the specifics of the functional requirements in the airline industry to determine if these might also have relevance for the other transportation domains.

Today, the vast transportation enterprise provides extremely large *static* data sets on location, status, condition, capacity, safety, and performance. Aviation information systems, which are at the forefront of technology, have several intrinsic distinctions. For instance, air traffic is continuously monitored and traffic situations and weather conditions are reported to aviators before they takeoff, as well as during their flight and landing segments. Also, electronic filing and amendment of flight plans and status enable the Federal Aviation Administration (FAA) to generate composite air traffic situation information and share that data with airlines on a minute-to-minute basis. Various communication channels make flight arrival and departure information available. The airline computer reservation and scheduling systems, in terms of size, complexity and effectiveness, offer great marketing advantages.

All of these benefit airline operations, but if attention is drawn to the travelers, the system of systems needs much improvement. Travelers have limited access to current information about travel options, costs, schedule/travel time, and traffic conditions. Static signs and schedules, mentioned earlier, along with radio announcements, citizens band radio chatter, and unexpected encounters with travel delays and missed connections due to various conditions are the only means by which the travelers come to know what is at hand today. Congestion, as we know from various reports, plagues the airways; twenty-three major airports experience over 20,000 hours of flight delay each year [14]. Consistent with its preeminent role, the airlines should then examine issues critical to more advanced information systems and their applications to offer the vast traveling populations improved transportation service, cost, safety, and efficiency! They should be evaluating a system innovation which:

- Issues "travel-cast" information based on actual conditions rather than on forecasts based on *static* schedules and/or historical patterns.

- Links multiple information sources (through the World Wide Web application enhancement on the Internet) that provide pre-trip travel information to people at home, work, and other sites where trips originate. With such options, travelers can make informed decisions regarding travel and traffic conditions, best departure time, weather patterns that spot safety risks or incipient hazards, terminals, access points, costs, timetables, and other alternatives.

- Provides online access to information—again through the WWW on the Internet—on travel services and facilities such as the location, operating hours, and availabilityof lodging, food, fuel, parking, motor vehicle repair, towing, medical, and other emergency services.

- Improves processing and distribution of flight arrival and departure data when flights are delayed due to weather or other factors.

- Facilitates seamless intermodal applications of Electronic Data Interchange (EDI) that includes invoicing and bills of lading, shipping, and order taking.

- Improves human resources management system for large international airlines. One common characteristic of the transportation industry is that its employees are highly mobile. It is important for carriers to know the location and status of their people and have them maintain contact with the central dispatch without any unwarranted delays or interruptions.

Successful innovations in the airline industry or, for that matter, in the transportation arena depend on whether timely, reliable information and meaningful services can be provided to transportation users. Are key technologies evident? Are joint technology initiatives needed in such areas as acquiring, accessing, and employing new products and services?

A partnership of several airlines—Apollo Travel Services—in which United has a majority ownership, is geared toward changing the way customers think about flying and, of course, about United in particular. This airline is the industry's market leader. It is on the forefront of applying information technology to its business. It is working to facilitate and provide customers with electronic libraries of information helpful to travelers interested in customs and other information about their destination.

REVIEW

If an airline is to survive its turbulent competitive wars, then it must strategically innovate products and services in every facet of its business, from passenger to aircraft parking to operations.

Unisys has a blueprint that uses some of the most advanced technology and techniques available. AeroMexico, as a global representative of the entire industry, is currently testing a component of the Unisys' Airport 2000 product. The component—the Airport Passenger Processing System or APPS [15]—is a very useful tool to display flight and other urgent information such as flight numbers, scheduled and estimated arrival and departure times, gate assignments, and special messages. These messages can further redirect passengers and agents to a new gate assignment. These types of information programming can satisfy multiple objectives, including notifying passenger of important messages. Unisys' APPS is, of course, just one of the products for total airline automation. But the system demonstrates what it means to look to technology as savior in the competitive wars. American and United know this only too well. From United's Airport of the Future in Philadelphia to Unisys' Airport 2000, the common denominator is the technology. And the bottom line is who can serve the customer better in the areas that are important. In that quest, other airlines also value information technology with its attendant innovation(s) and have been examining more seriously and more specifically the Internet options for:

> **Marketing and Advertising (Vacations)**—To create demand through Newsgroups, and also to make information available for browsing, including audio and video 'samples' of favorite destinations: Florida, Colorado, San Juan, The Bahamas, Cancun, the London Show Tour

> **Frequent Traveler Awards**—To electronically process orders for the rules and information about membership, program enrollment, requesting awards, redeeming awards, mileage statements, etc.

> **Delivering Products and Services**—To allow customers to download schedules, pricing, and special fares and services information including passenger travel for individuals and groups, cargo, PDQ packages, charters, the hub airport maps, routes in the U.S.A. and international destinations, the fleet etc.

Partnering, Integration, Consumer Prospecting, and Advertising

This discussion remains incomplete until we also question how the innovations in the Internet challenge both the public and private enterprises to create new models for partnership. For instance, California Department of Transportation (Caltrans) has formed a teaming agreement with Maxwell Laboratories to provide the public an opportunity to access real-time traffic information via the World Wide Web. A superimposed graphical display on a San Diego freeway map, as well as a text listing display up-to-the-minute freeway speeds, accident reports, and construction closures. Red, yellow, and green indicate the congestion severity. Further instructions are also made available via Internetmail request at: traffic_info@scubed.com. [16].

The advantages of the Internet products and services are also being actively sought by the overnight delivery services to complement the "just-in-time" logistics requirements associated with their customer/supplier support, geographic reach/general accessibility, and specific and detailed information about the status of shipments in transit. Their functional requirements echo the general theme of the transportation enterprise:

- Timebased competitive advantage

- Productivity improvement through Internet usage strategy

- On-demand linkage with customers and suppliers

- New kinds of business network (virtual alliance)

- Reaching new markets through greater speed, efficiency, and safety

FedEx provided customer service with personal computers and free tracking software for almost ten years. It allowed the customers access to their infrastructure and private network. FedEx realizes that today's customer behavior is different. Robert Hamilton, FedEx manager of information services marketing says, "customer behavior...includes public online environments as a place where business is being conducted." [17]

To stay ahead of the trend, FedEx offers its tracking software and shipping information online. It has proven to be a very popular service—more than 2,800 software packages were downloaded in the first month the software was made available online. Although the software enables customers to track airbills about 6,000 times a day; this Web service is not now the primary way people track FedEx packages. What is interesting is that there is a steady flow of people who use the Web site to track packages, and they are also visiting other areas of the FedEx Web site to learn more about the company. The company receives thousands of E-Mail messages and surprisingly few complaints. Based on the experiences to date, FedEx believes the Internet will become even more important for business. Hamilton hastens to add that some of the driving forces in today's business world are doing business through the Internet, and those who come back to the site "are doing business in novel ways."

Similarly, other corporations are gathering information from the same critical resource: their customers. If this is an attempt to understand and appreciate what business people want and then bring in the technology, the process adds value to the enterprise's products and services. This meshing of business and technology demonstrates how enterprises can better leverage their technology investments. So what you—as the CFO, CIO, or CEO — ought to be addressing or doing is "Justifying Technology's Value to the Bottom Line." This theme was the primary topic in a recent conference in New York City [18].

Environmental Monitoring and the Internet

Remember *EXXON Valdez*, the supertanker that ran aground in the Gulf of Alaska? Authorities were informed of the mishap and a management team, experienced in oil spill emergencies, was summoned to assess the situation. The team requested an aerial reconnaissance of the region asking that the airplane observations be distributed in real-time to a team of environmental experts located in various cities in the United States. The experts announced that the rate of spillage and spread of the oil was a major environmental disaster in the making.

Now consider this:

SCENARIO

> Within minutes, the emergency team will determine via online databases the resources available in the local area to combat the oil spill, including ships, personnel, and equipment. However, the scientific experts must also remotely access supercomputing centers to utilize advanced, high-resolution, numerical models that will allow them to predict the likely path of the oil spill. This method of prediction, along with satellite imaging essential to monitoring and supporting the spill containment operations on a broad scale, will allow them to minimize environmental damage by focusing on oil spill containment and clean-up operations. Now, suppose the experts are able to access and invoke the remote computational centers, thanks to easy and timely access via a technologically feasible internetworking environment. Under this scenario, the experts have real-time and historical observation data, advanced computational facilities, online databases, communications networks to link observing systems to emergency managers and, in this instance, they just may be able to marshall all the resources in time to avoid serious, long-term damage to the area's environment and economy.

In today's environment, we have the ability to take all kinds of measurements, but a fundamental problem is coping with the avalanche of data emanating from widely diverse systems, stored and disseminated in varied formats, and acquired in support of different enterprises' missions. Therefore, a related issue is whether or not there are technological solutions to transmit large volumes of disparate data so that users can retrieve them from databases and manipulate them. After all, businesses require environmental information to make critical decisions that directly affect their productivity and overall competitiveness.

REVIEW

Do agricultural companies and small farming concerns need environmental information to plan future planting and harvesting and to assess market needs, especially after floods, droughts, insect infestation, and plant disease diagnosis?

Does the construction industry need ongoing assessment of regional and local environmental conditions?

Do electric power utilities need environmental information to plan fuel consumption and anticipate power outages for reasons such as solar activity, severe storms, or geologic activity?

Does the insurance industry require information to set insurance rates and assess potential risks for, let us say, a property near hazardous materials sites, earthquake zones, or flood plains?

Can consultants and other private sector companies benefit from value-added information products to advise commodity traders?

Can the trucking industry benefit from the latest information on hazards from a wide range of sources and its ready dissemination via the Internet for contingency planning to arrange local and distant deliveries?

The federal government is primarily responsible for environmental monitoring; however, as evident from the preceding issues and questions, private enterprises need technologies for observing the environment, and providing value-added services and other additional information products.

National Aeronautic and Space Administration (NASA) has a program on Public Use of Earth and Space Science Data over the Internet. This is a pilot program developed to demonstrate digital library technologies that include:

- Heterogeneous databases

- Information retrieval

- Advanced search and browse techniques

- Data structures

- Data and image compression

- Direct public access to satellite imagery and a host of other tools and techniques; and

application and accessibility of earth and space science databases that include:

- Atmospheric, oceanic, and land monitoring

- Agriculture

- Forestry

- Transportation

- Aquaculture

- Mineral exploration

- Land-use planning

- Cartography

- Entertainment

- Environmental hazards monitoring, and so forth

The Environmental Protection Agency (EPA) disseminates information through its electronic bulletin boards as well as other means to the interested stakeholders. Its Toxic Release Inventory (TRI) is a key environmental system.

One of the Department of Energy's (DOE) main objectives is to leverage the large, ongoing investment made by industry as well as government agencies in the successful implementation of the internet working infrastructure. DOE maintains that its agencies must have high performance access to monitoring and modeling resources. It adds that these resources are required to validate remediation plans and, through that process, reduce the time required for actual remediation of the environmental problems and issues. Therefore,

DOE wants to enhance productivity and competitiveness in the environmental restoration industry by allowing environmental industry enterprises access to information on regulatory matters in a timely manner.

There are several other interagency efforts underway that are equally valid and purposeful for rapid response for emergency action in the event of natural or man-made environmental disaster. The Global Change Data and Information System, the National Spatial Data Infrastructure, the High Performance Computing and Communications Program, and other programs address topics such as:

- geologic processes (including earthquakes) and earth resources

- biological habitats, resources, and diversity

- past environmental change in the physical, chemical, and biological record

- geography and cartography

- polar and arid region processes

- ecosystem modeling and dynamics

It is vitally important for environmental enterprises—large or small—to access many levels of data and maintain extensive collaborations across many organizational and technical barriers, nationally and internationally.

Information Access/Connectivity (Including International); Exploiting Acquired and Processed Environmental Data

Based on the mission and environment of your enterprise, you must then probe further:

REVIEW

Will your enterprise benefit from a network that includes high performance technologies, advanced distributed capabilities, real-time data flows, and accounting capabilities to support requirements for management of energy- and environment-related product or service demand, supply, and delivery?

Is your enterprise responsible for broadcasting warnings, or emergency bulletins that reach the intended target population in a reliable and timely manner? Do you need robust and dependable transmission media for data that affect protection of life and property?

These issues are applicable across all energy- and environment-related industry operations, such as electric, gas, and water utilities. There is a multiplicity of databases, and many of these are maintained by individual facilities, industrial users, interconnected utilities, independent power generators, or transmission facility operators. Most data resident in these databases are needed for disaster response activities. As an environmental enterprise, you should consider the following options:

REVIEW

Are you confronting major problems in the integration of heterogeneous databases?

Do you view the Internet as a likely integrating medium to access real-time databases, to address emergency responses, facilities planning, facilities management, and maintenance?

Does your activity entail the use of Electronic Data Interchange (EDI)?

THE PARADIGM SHIFT

Charles Feld, IS executive of Frito-Lay Inc., identifies management's role as that of "defining the IT requirements, making the business case for the new systems, and harvesting the benefits by measuring and reporting the business value of IT." [19] In IS projects that involve complexity and state-of-the-art technology, it is difficult, if not impossible, to state clear, concise, and complete requirements. The preceding paragraphs examined a variety of enterprises in terms of:

- an accelerating rate of change in their particular business environments;

- an exponential rate of change in information technologies, as these technologies become integrated to create a new layer of connectivity among all information technology networks, giving rise to the Internet;

- the crucial role of the Internet for effectiveness of the enterprise overall.

We want to ask the right questions of people who know the business environment and how it is evolving, and who can gauge the evolution of customer needs and perceptions, competitor effectiveness in satisfying those needs and perceptions, and opportunities and threats from other sources. Many business failures are attributable to the lack of detailed understanding of its functional requirements. Therefore, a process must be instituted for enterprise analysis, environmental analysis, and strategic synthesis. This process is not an action plan with prescriptive steps; it is interaction leading to a shared understanding and direction that produces results. It must be driven by the chief executive to ensure that the right people are involved in the right way to address the relevant issues or questions. Among other things, this means that we must focus on those 20 percent of activities that determine 80 percent of the enterprise's effectiveness [20]. This direction-setting planning or exercise requires a sophisticated understanding of:

- the enterprise,

- its missions,

- the business it is in and why,

- the customer of those businesses and their needs, and

- the competitors seeking to satisfy similar needs.

The CEO, CFO, or CIO can make the greatest impact at this planning level. The questions were purposely designed to force the top executives to focus on a strategic vision—a view of the future that is at once challenging and achievable. If they understand these questions in terms of their functional requirements and identify uses of the Internet in pursuit of objectives at their level, then this section has served as a touchstone for employees at every level.

For years, the long-range information systems plan was based primarily on a set of application development projects. In consideration of workload and price/performance parameters, there had always been incremental action plans to keep the technology environment current through acquisition of computers, peripherals, and system software. These plans rarely received scrutiny outside of the IS department of the various enterprises and their direct executive leadership. The environment is different today. Application development projects continue to be important in many instances, but now competitive forces are generating a need for an enterprisewide information technology project with the

Internet serving as a backbone communications network. This increases the user community's ability to keep its support systems current with rapidly changing business conditions with little direct support from the IS department. Empowering every enterprise user is the new approach!

Chapter **3**

The High Performance Business Team

"*As organizations reach for a global presence, they need major help managing their important information, and giving their employees, vendors, and business partners timely and efficient access to that information. But it isn't a robust search capability alone that brings success. The real key is the quality of the indexing architecture. By using...Web Search Server tool kit and other application,.developers can build a tightly-integrated, high performance index, equipped with the intelligence to understand and respond to queries...that will help enterprises get their information in order, and ease the transition into the larger, online environment.*"

Tom Jenkins, president of Open Text.

Source: "Open Text's Web Search Server for OEMs; Offers Unique Intelligent Search Capabilities For the Internet and Enterprise-Wide Webs," *Business Wire*, New York, September 21, 1995.

BUILDING THE HIGH PERFORMANCE IS FUNCTION

Now that you know about the various applications and tools of the Internet, and why enterprises are using it, hopefully you:

1) understand the realities of the Internet; and

2) appreciate the trends affecting your particular business concern.

As a reality check, we should note that the excitement and hype are not yet over, but the initial wave of commercial Internet development is. You can see the presence of major vendors, and even second and third-tier players are on board. Internet conference speakers no longer ask Are you on board? Rather, they want to know How can you exploit this opportunity [1]? That is our point of departure. It is time for you to review the goals, objectives, and performance needs of the various business units within your enterprise. This will help you decide which Internet tools and resources to use, and which to emphasize.

Not all aspects of the Internet environment will be feasible or desirable for every enterprise, but a survey of each business unit will help you identify some common elements that apply to their choice of specific Internet programs and facilities for their own business environments and, in turn, to the enterprise as a whole. In general, every business unit will want the following capabilities:

- Access to Information: Access for more individuals to information and assistance in organizing and presenting the information.

- Resource Management: An information system without specialized staff and maintenance overhead, but with a consistent and lucid interface to facilitate online support for user training, access to other users, remote diagnostics, and problem resolution.

- Partnership and Collaboration: Collaboration with a variety of partners both within and outside of a business function for greater productivity and effectiveness.

- Diversity: Ability to serve an increasingly diverse population.

The Forrester Report [2] advocates the formation of a flexible and dynamic Internet group comprising, marketing, operations, lines of business, executive staff, and IT. One person, preferably a high-level executive from marketing, not the CIO, should head the company's

Internet team. This person should have a broad-based understanding of the customer, products, and distribution. She or he should help identify, document, and produce a quantifiable index to justify a given business function's, and, in turn, the whole enterprise's presence on the Internet. With the help of colleagues from the various divisions, she/he will compile information on each division's needs. Each division and function will address separately and individually if it:

- Markets primarily to customers with income over $60,000
- Advertises heavily
- Requires extensive customer feedback

- Requires 7 X 24 X 365 service
- Maintains worldwide customer service
- Maintains a large network (over 200) of suppliers

- Sells "bits"—information, equities, banking, software, etc.
- Sells worldwide
- Does direct marketing or catalog selling

- Needs extensive intracompany E-Mail
- Has high end user pressure for Internet access
- Requires that be provided for its employees with an external exposure

- Has many users with a research focus
- Operates in a science-oriented business (e.g., energy)
- Conducts extensive competitive analysis

Based on the number of items checked, an initial index can be derived to identify any particular division's Internet needs. If we follow Forrester's methodological guidelines, one way of codifying the responses might be:

Total of Responses	**Internet deployment needs**
0-3	No urgency
4-8	Internet pilot useful at this stage
8+	Immediate full-scale Internet rollout warranted

Based on an individual's personal knowledge and preferences, this could be a purely subjective assessment. The author is not advocating the use of this methodology or, for that matter, any other single methodology. The underlying concern here is to facilitate each division's responses so that they are able to articulate their particular business needs in terms of:

Information

- Retrieval/Research/Summary/Industry Index
— Marketing surveys
— Consumer surveys
— New and differentiated services

Communications

- External through the World Wide Web
- Internal through the Web

Marketing

- Business to business marketing
- Consumer marketing

Sales/Advertising

- Online sales
- Distribution channels
- Information for vendors/customers on:

—Product, Dealer Names and Locations, Product Support Services, Map showing how to get to the company headquarters, etc.

Data Transfer

- Product Support
- Collaborative Product Development
- Electronic Commerce/EDI

Logistics

- Scheduling
- Planning
- Calendars
- Inventory Management

Alternative Communications for Cost Containment

• Reduced hot line expenses

• Less wasted time and frustration from telephone tags

• Lower printing and distribution costs for manuals, technical bulletins, etc.

• More effective use of repair personnel

In initial identification of business needs there is no need to do a "bottom line" assessment. The responses given by each division must be fine tuned, and the Internet plans also need to mature. The author advocates the use of a comprehensive format in which marketing, operations, purchasing, government affairs, training, human resources, legal affairs, and other divisions in a major enterprise are given the authority to voice their concerns and suggestions on the above questions and issues. The individuals representing a division should include:

• Line of business managers who are considering an interactive commercial presence on the Internet

• Management, including legal affairs and human resources, who want to understand and assess the importance of the Internet to their businesses and what must be done to safeguard the interests of the enterprise

• Management who are interested in electronic commerce including online ordering or sales

• Project managers who need to understand the business and technical requirements involved in Internet development

• Technical managers who are charged with creating a development infrastructure for future projects

Their immediate task should be to review and document the division's mission, goals, objectives, and growth strategy. In an exercise of this nature, each participant will have an opportunity to gain a significant awareness about the "big picture"—that is, how each group contributes to a common enterprisewide concept development.

Subsequent to that exercise they would be better equipped to suggest, with help from the leader of the Internet team,

- Places where the Internet will assist their business/operating divisions

- Internet tools and resources to use

- Critical success factors for Internet-based projects, including management, business, and technical building blocks that could enable convergence and interoperation of Internet services/applications

They should then commence work on a roadmap to reach the enterprise's goal. Each participant will have a different awareness as to what Internet service or application will be best suited for their respective functional areas. However, the joint effort will yield comprehensive strategies which will impact the whole enterprise that they may not otherwise think through, including risk, cost, and investment factors.

A format is comprehensive when it asks the participants to address several different options including: return on investment; development, deployment, support, and training resources for the Internet and its internetworking technologies and applications; development of interfaces between divisions/organizations within their enterprise; and tools for developing such interfaces. It is through those interfaces, that an Internet presence will be developed.

Based on recent studies [3], one can infer that Internet-related activities take anywhere between six to twenty-four months to become profitable, depending upon the level and cost of the activity [4]. A full-node installation might be profitable only after two or three years, depending on the cost and increase in business. The fundamental issue is that there is much to be gained by leveraging the Internet for competitive advantage. On the other hand, how aggressive should one be for the growth and evolution of the enterprise wide Internet? The Internet team leader has to facilitate this kind of a comprehensive strategy assessment. To that end, a format is helpful, especially one that allows the:

a) respective organizational representatives to address all points including return on investments;

b) initiation and development of a consensus-driven approach.

In attempting to assess the return on investments, the team will have the added responsibility of evaluating time lines for developing online applications for deployment on the Internet. The author submits that the following format will produce relevant insights as we attempt to derive ratings of importance for potential Internet benefits.

FORMAT

Characteristics of the current business environment

A. Operational Environment *(reference the particular business environment)*

B. Functions/Activities

C. Performance/Interface Requirements

Purpose to be served by the Internet services and applications

A. Potential organizational environment *(describe operational scenarios at a high level—how, and for what business functions, the users plan to exploit the Internet capabilities. A scenario may include one or more of the following: competitive analysis, communication, financial transactions, marketing and promotion, sales and distribution, customer support, business and economic statistics, newsgroups, and so forth)*

B. Internet services in the context of specific business functions

—User
—Mission
—How
—Why

Impact

A. Improvements to core processes

B. Support and commitment costs

Strategy recommendations

A. High Growth

B. Low Growth

Suppose the Internet team leader advises the purchasing, legal affairs, or marketing division's representative to use this format and inform other divisional representatives as to how the Internet will be used by his or her functional area. Regardless of who is targeted first, the representative will apply the conventional concerns he or she is used to in the given functional area. For instance, marketing will address: marketing process, new product, and market research. Furthermore, in evaluating Internet marketing strategies, the usual indicators will also be weighed:

- market potential

- market forecast

- sales potential

- sales forecast

- market share

- customer needs

- non-customer needs, and so forth

Business functions in any given enterprise are likely to have in place the basic competence in doing what they do. But if they plan to leap to the next level, that is, the so called paradigm shift that the Internet affords, they will address the question What do we do now? They will inevitably review the concerns identified above—but this time, their focus shifts to realizing benefits from cross-functional integration and/or from working together for continuous improvement.

Using the format suggested above, any other functional area can state the characteristics of the current environment. They then proceed to articulate the benefits to be accrued through Internet-based marketing. In the following, we compose a hypothetical response for an airline marketing division to address the various sections outlined in the above format.

ABC Airlines Marketing Division

Characteristics of the current business environment

A. Operational Environment

The marketing department is responsible for the company's strategic and tactical objectives. Strategic objectives include key city focus, strategic initiatives for a particular year, and long-range plans. All of these objectives affect the types and range of marketing options and the market segments the division can consider. These options cover scheduled services, and fare discount offerings as a marketing tool; similarly, market segments cover tours, holiday markets, and other such cuts.

B. Functions/Activities

The marketing division's major concern is to develop products that appeal to the traveling population served by the particular airline. The product is a flight, with the appropriate mix of classes, fares, and services for the particular markets that the company wishes to serve on the route(s) in question. Some of the critical functions that marketing has to address include: appropriate customer service to deliver products in a smooth and efficient manner, short-term changes to the company's product, the product mix in each flight to generate revenue through traffic, and a richer yield mix. These functions produce a complex flow and exchange of information with many company divisions (such as a pricing division which updates and announces fare schedule changes numerous times a day) and external organizations, particularly travel agents and other airlines.

C. Performance/Interface Requirements

Appropriate customer services require that if the marketing decides to make changes in flight schedules for any reason, it must promptly announce those changes to the passengers and keep them up-to-date on the status of any delay. Good customer service for an airline company also means the ability to provide real-time information on:

- Flight-time changes (delays)
- Seat availability
- Reservations by name
- Special accommodations/requests (e.g., wheel chair)

- Boarding gates allocated

- In-flight services available

- Aircraft type etc.

Purpose to be served by the Internet services and application

A. Potential organizational environment

Starting with the end in mind, today's marketers are paying more attention to the customer's needs.They are making technology investments to improve quality, customer service, flexibility, and speed. In the commercial airline industry, customer loyalty is the most valuable long-term asset. In this environment, true customer intimacy is earnestly sought by airline marketing executives. They believe that they can cultivate intimacy by being able to deliver on-the-spot local information.

There are efforts under way to capture and integrate with the reservation system information on how many times an individual has flown or how much money he or she has spent to get preferential treatment in terms of seat selection and fare levels. For example, American Airlines, Sabre Group's parent company, realizes that reservation agents could utilize such information. Accordingly, the company has designed a special section on the AMR Internet Home Page to meet the needs of its travel agency subscribers, referred to as the Central Reservation System's (CRS) "customers" or "partners." [5]

American Airline's Internet offering goes beyond this. It is designed to serve four distinct markets: Sabre Group's travel distribution partners (airlines, hotels, car rental companies, and other travel suppliers), travel agencies, corporate travelers, and independent travelers. There are several notable features on American Airline's Internet Home Page. All of them are clearly targeted toward one or more of the markets. For instance, the What's New section promotes special offers and new products and services. In addition, there is information relative to:

- Baggage requirements and handling

- American Airlines city ticketing offices

- Duty-free shopping

- American Airlines aircraft specifications

- Cities served by jet

- Ticket delivery services

- Airport profiles, complete with maps, for eight facilities in the U.S.

- American Eagle, the regional subsidiary

- FlyAAway Vacations

- Frequent flyer programs, including airport lounge information

One of the best customer services would be on online booking function over the Internet. Southwest, USAir, and several other airlines are working toward the development of such capability [6]. With such efforts under way, it is clear that the airline marketing experts are now bent on using the Internet to get data to—and on—the customer. In a study conducted by INPUT Inc., the potential Internet benefits were rank ordered to make explicit preferences for new customer focus. Table 3.1 illustrates the point.

Potential Internet Benefit	Consolidated Rating
Delivering more information	4.4
Receiving feedback from customers	4.3
Enhancing relationship with customers	4.2
Responding more quickly to customers	4.2
Delivering sales information less expensively	4.1

Source: "Internet Sales and Marketing Directions," Report from INPUT's Internet Opportunities Program, 1995.

Table 3.1 Ratings of Importance of Potential Internet Benefits

Number of Responses = 64 (1 = "Not Important," 5 = "Very Important")

Potential Internet Benefit	Consolidated Rating
Promoting products through new media	4.1
Adding new sales channels	4.0
Providing better sales information	4.0
Obtaining new customers	4.0
Supporting customers less expensively	3.8
Targeting individuals	3.8
Testing new sales strategies	3.6

Source: "Internet Sales and Marketing Directions," Report from
INPUT's Internet Opportunities Program, 1995.

Table 3.1 Ratings of Importance of Potential Internet Benefits (Continued)

Forward thinking airlines also see the Internet facilities as tools that offer them a competitive edge by providing more access to customers, and therefore, more access to their dollars. Mexicana, Cathay Pacific, and Virgin Atlantic are experimenting with some of these Internet applications; similarly, other airlines and travel related companies are investigating applications such as electronic data interchange (EDI), efficient customer response, and point-of-sales data mining to improve operations both internally and externally. For example, Radisson Hospitality Worldwide has a system by which a customer, booking a room on the Internet, will receive confirmation by E-Mail. This is a strategic move by Radisson to capture between 30 million and 40 million users worldwide, plus another 100,000 new users expected each week on the Internet [7].

B. Internet services in the context of specific business functions

---

CAUTION

The intent here is to demonstrate a possible approach by a marketing function to justify new and differentiated services with the help of the Internet infrastructures. The listings of the applications below should not be construed as definitive recommendations for any airline or travel related company's marketing functions.

USER:	Marketing Division
No. 1 Mission	Promotional Fares, Executive Clubs, Fly Away Vacations, Customer Questionnaire, Market Analysis of Internet Users
HOW:	Home Page
WHY:	The Home Page and its associated files can be used as a vehicle to promote the company, its affiliates, and their services. There could be multiple pages of information within this site. Linked pages could describe: (a) the company's products for agencies that focus on leisure or business travel markets; (b) negotiation of corporate travel accounts; (c) travel industry trends, from the retailer's point of view; (d) destination information, including local transportation services, connections, currency rates, appropriate dress, holidays, geography, and embassy addresses; (e) special offers and new products and services; (f) baggage requirements and handling; (g) aircraft specifications; (h) airport profiles, complete with maps, for certain facilities; (i) frequent flyer programs, including airport lounge information, and so forth. Also, a comment form and a frequent flyers enrollment form could be designed to solicit information from the customers. Figure 3.1 is an illustration of an airline's Home Page.

USER:	Marketing Division
No. 2 Mission	Marketing Services—Consumer Correspondence
HOW:	UseNet
WHY:	To leverage Internet's infrastructure to reach millions of customers and prospects worldwide and serve as a dynamic communication and collaboration medium between the company and the customers, thereby turning the network into the ultimate business weapon of the 21st century.
No. 3 Mission	Frequent Traveler (FT) Account Access, Frequent Traveler Award
HOW:	Electronic Data Interchange (EDI)
WHY:	To manage FT account inquiry processing more effectively and in less time. A tremendous volume of paper documents flows between the traveler and the unit responsible for the FT program. The process of creating the FT statement, mailing it or sending information by fax, and re-keying is quite wasteful. EDI has had considerable success, with over 30,000 U.S. corporations currently using it. Internet EDI provides the basis for a comprehensive electronic FT program solution.

Impact

A. Improvements to core processes

In addition to the above specific applications, the Internet could be a great facilitator of general, day-to-day business communications. Many examples of this are already extant, and a vast number more are possible. A few common examples:

- E-Mail can assist in keeping the lines of communication open between marketing and among people at all levels. Ongoing relationships are facilitated, and problems can be resolved before they become critical.

- The management of special projects—up-to-the-minute schedule information—can be instantly made available to all involved parties.

| Flying | Business | Leisure | News | Americas |

| Frequent Flyer | The Qantas Club | Freight | Regional Airlines |

| Reservations | Schedules | Arrivals & Departures | Survey | Index |

Welcome aboard Qantas, The Australian Airline. Whether you're flying within Australia, or travelling the world, Qantas can help you get there in style and comfort. So, before you take off, take a flight around this site. It's been designed to help you organise your travel with us, send freight, or simply learn about our history.

For our worldwide customers outside North America,please click here

AMAZIA SERVICES

Our Qantas North American Web Site is managed by Amazia Services. For more information about Amazia and their wide range of services click here.

 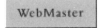

Legal Information, Copyright (c) Qantas Airways Ltd. 1996

Source: http://www.qa.com

Figure 3.1 Sample Home Page for an airline

B. Support and commitment costs

Based on a review of the various study reports, marketing makes the following observations:

- Fortune 1,000 companies are moving toward the Internet with low-cost, multidisciplinary efforts.

- A Web cost is hard to report, because it is difficult to quantify the time of all the individuals involved, and add those figures to the hardware and software expenses that are more commonly available.

- Marketing can either be done in-house or the whole thing can be out-sourced.

- If we do want to commit to a figure, either way it would cost around $76,000.

- Technology is not the real issue; rather, the learning process associated with understanding a new distribution channel is of utmost importance.

- Major commitments to the network call for additional support for proper security.

Strategy Recommendations

A. High Growth

The productivity analysis can be based on "hard" numbers such as revenue, labor costs, and capital costs. However, marketing perceives the immediate need to invest in "soft" benefits such as customer service, as opposed to a hard-nosed, bottom-line orientation toward cost-cutting. It observes that the customer-oriented companies recently had the best productivity performance. Figure 3.2 documents the evidence.

Marketing further underscores that the Internet is changing everything, including telecommunications costs, business practices, and industry structures. It concurs with the Hambrecht and Quist analysts: "the expanding opportunity of the Internet today engenders a business strategy in the industry to "get big fast," where profits and revenues are less important than establishing widespread presence." [8] Based on further competitor analysis [refer to Vis, D. "AMR Lands on the Internet with Expansive Airline Site," *Travel Weekly*, Volume 54, Number 41, May 25, 1995.], marketing recommends a High Growth strategy.

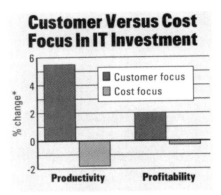

Profitability is measured as pretax return on assets

*% change in moving from the median of the low group (e.g., low customer service focus) to the median of the high group (e.g., high customer focus)

Data: MIT/INFORMATIONWEEK

Source: "The Productive Keep Producing," MIT's InformationWeek 500 Study, *INFORMATIONWEEK*, September 18, 1995, p. 43

Figure 3.2 Customer Versus Cost Focus in IT Investment

B. Low Growth

Does not apply.

The Internet is relevant to all major divisions of an enterprise of all sizes and in virtually every industry. Moreover, there could be specific, high-value Internet applications in just about all business functions. Following the example set forth for an airline marketing division, the various functions such as purchasing, advertising, customer service, public and community relations, investor relations, training, human resources, legal affairs, tax, pricing, inventory control, and engineering could all make compelling arguments to justify and install Internet applications. Media invariably directs our attention to the "futures," but just so everybody knows, it is entirely feasible for the various business functions today to use a broad spectrum of Internet applications.

- E-Mail offers a solution to telephone tag—Internet can integrate an enterprise's E-Mail systems with those of its customers.

- Electronic forms capabilities go beyond E-Mail and insure that a customer is directed to the specific information needed to address the problem most efficiently.

- Internet tightens links needed for inventory control functions. It is beginning to emerge as a very useful functional environment for information management, distribution, and collaboration computing. There are special applications that allow multiple simultaneous executions of various functions, including innovative gathering, scheduling, and monitoring with highest possible performance [9].

- Status information of various types can be shared via electronic mail and bulletin board-like capabilities.

- Securities and Exchange Commission (SEC) filings can be monitored through SEC's online electronic data gathering and retrieval operations, investor brochures, and alerts.

- Legislative actions and other congressional proceedings.

- Requests for bids, industry standards and specifications, patent and trademark information, international trade information, etc.

- Contract negotiations via the Internet are efficient and allow draft languages to be exchanged with greater speed and finalized rapidly.

- Legal issues can be addressed through a comprehensive collection of law materials now available on the Internet. As the Internet expands and the amount of information mushrooms, Internet vendors are showing the users where the really good information is. For instance, the recently launched LAWLinks directs users to numerous federal and state government Internet locations. These locations could be at the Library of Congress, Department of Justice, or at the new White House server. It also arranges legal resources by legal practice area, and has access to a variety of Inter net archives, electronic mail lists, databases, and search tools.

Again, the major facilities that provide the actual Internet communication links to the users via document creation, simultaneous publication, access, or retrieval functions are E-Mail, FTP, WWW, USENET, and TELNET. Each function within an enterprise's business areas needs to assess its particular performance needs in the realm of:

- Customer support

- Multimedia

- Product reviews

- Promotional announcements

- Product flyers

- Surveys

- Vendor contacts

- Service evaluations, and so forth.

Then and then only will a functional entity be able to clearly assess and identify the Internet tools and resources that will:

- save money through better timing of investments related to changing business strategies and the subject enterprise's desired production capacity improvements;

- save money and time by knowing and understanding the strategies of third party vendors so that their innovations and products can be leveraged to further the enterprise and its business areas;

- save money and time by accessing an experience base of business practices concerning product announcement, flyers, specifications, promotional notifications, catalogs, customer support, and service information;

- make available references to other "ongoing or previous negotiations" prior to decision-making on contracts;

- provide insights into challenges, business functions, directions, and strategies utilized by competitors and, therefore, will

- help develop better strategic plans and audit existing services against a library of credible market surveys, reviews, and comments.

The aggregation of the selected tools and resources by all the functions within several business areas will produce the necessary recommendations for a total enterprise to get things done. Figure 3.3 documents this selection matrix and depicts how the introduction of high performance Internet applications, tools, and facilities recasts external relationships and opens up the enterprise.

	E-Mail	Gopher	FTP	BBS	UseNet	WWW	WAIS
MARKETING	H	X	X	H	H	H	H
PURCHASING	H	H	H	X	X	L	X
CUSTOMER SERVICE	H	H	H	H		H	H
LEGAL AFFAIRS	H	H	H	X	H	X	X
HUMAN RESOURCES	H	H	X	X		X	X
ADVERTISING	H	H	X	H	H	H	X
INVESTOR RELATIONS	H	H	H	L	X	X	X
GOVERNMENT AFFAIRS	H	H	H	X	H	H	X
PRICING	H	X	H	X	H		X
ENGINEERING	H	H	H		H	X	X
ADMINISTRATION	H			H	H	L	X

Legend: L = Limited Usefullness or Access; X = Useful; H = Major Source

Figure 3.3 Technique to Document Internet Tool Selection

Chapter **4**

Taking New Measures

John Chiazza prepared himself for his first meeting with Eastman Kodak Co.'s new chief financial officer. He presumed the first question would be How much was the company spending on information technology relative to revenue? He was prepared with data, charts, and spreadsheets. But the CFO's first question wasn't about IT-to-revenue ratios. Rather, the first thing he asked was, "Where are we using information technology to competitive advantage?" The cost issues did come up later, but the first unexpected question revealed that the days of relying solely on outmoded, traditional financial metrics to monitor the returns on IT investment appear to be on the wane...1994 marks the year the productivity paradox perished.

Source: E. B. Baatz, "Altered Stats," *CIO*, October 15, 1994, pp. 40-41.

VARIABLE COSTS

Deloitte & Touche Management Consulting Group conducted its Seventh Annual Survey of North American Chief Information Executives in 1995. Nearly 400 U.S. and Canadian CIOs, whose companies reported an annual net revenue from less than $100 million to more than $5 billion, responded to this survey. Figure 4.1 identifies the respondent companies by industry.

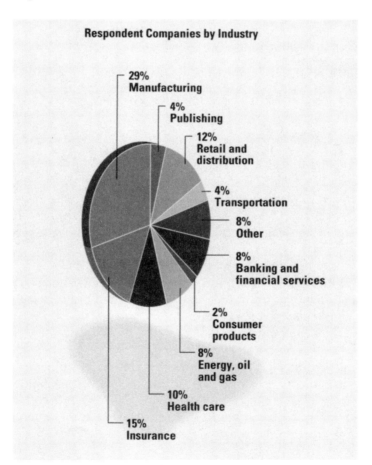

Respondent Companies by Industry

- 29% Manufacturing
- 4% Publishing
- 12% Retail and distribution
- 4% Transportation
- 8% Other
- 8% Banking and financial services
- 2% Consumer products
- 8% Energy, oil and gas
- 10% Health care
- 15% Insurance

Source: Information Technology Consulting Services, *Leading Trends in Information Services: Seventh Annual Survey of North American Chief Information Executives*—1995, Deloitte & Touche

Figure 4.1 Respondent Company by Industry

The survey findings show that the information services departments experienced an average budget increase of 3.5 percent a year during 1993-1994 [1]. Budgets vary widely from one industry to another when measured against employment as Figure 4.2 illustrates. Our intent is to examine what is driving these budget increases and how to account for the productivity improvements that the various companies may or may not experience due to their increased spending on information technology products and services. We will review if these companies are:

- Trying for better technological positioning relative to their peer companies.

- Seeking more information processing capabilities. If so, why?

- Enhancing their customer relations and market share.

- Seeking Internet information processing features.

We will then seek to analyze:

- Investment requirements for the Internet capabilities.

- Different options for measuring the benefits of standard information technology packages. Then we will evaluate if these options are suitable for measuring and quantifying the benefits of the Internet technology, specifically.

- Old financial ratios such as return on investment (ROI) and return on asset (ROA). We will assess if these ratios allow us to measure the productivity improvement made possible by the introduction of new information handling capabilities.

- Changes in program/project evaluations that can give us a better perspective on the potential return on investment on Internet technology.

- Project authorization bias in the ROI methodology, and if we should depart from the strict project authorization bias.

- Finally, we seek to find an index to help us determine productivity improvement in an entire enterprise vis-a-vis a single project or a business function within the enterprise.

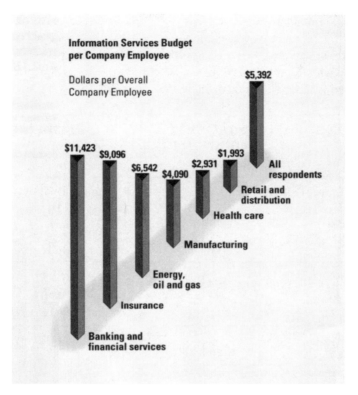

Source: Information Technology Consulting Services, Leading Trends in Information Services: Seventh Annual Survey of North American Chief Information Executives—1995, Deloitte & Touche LLP Management Consulting, 1995.

Figure 4.2 Information Services Budget per Company Employee

INFORMATION IMPERATIVE

Technical positioning has an immediacy in business circles. In just about every facet of business today, the guiding principle is "Time is money." Market opportunities surface and then disappear in the blink of an eye, and corporations realize that the customers go to the company that provides the best service and support. Their leverage puts the onus on the corporations to react quickly. Translated into day-to-day business functional and performance requirements, that means corporations must have easy access to the right information and the ability to transmit that information.

The Internet, as we have noted earlier, makes interactions with buyers, sellers, and competitors/colleagues faster, cheaper, and more intelligent. A corporate-surfer, for instance, can get on the Net and quickly head off rumors, pick up marketing leads, elevate company visibility, get a feel for industry trends, and locate valuable data sources. Table 4.1 documents the results of a survey of 114 respondents on the primary reasons for current Internet activity. Efficiency and effectiveness of communications are clearly of utmost importance, followed by the potential for increase in business.

REASON	FREQUENCY OF MENTION (%)	SPECIFIC ATTRACTION
Create efficiency and effective communications	33	• Wide, global network • Another medium for customer contact • Electronic mail
Increase business	20	• Access to a huge pool of potential customers • New access to existing customers
Enhance company image	14	• "Obvious place to be" • "Everyone is doing it" • Need to keep up with the competition
Keep current with technology	14	• "Testing the waters" • Keep up-to-date with the next level of communication • "Wave of the future"
Access new information	9	• Massive amounts of information available for research and general information purposes
Enhance customer service	7	• Expand avenues of access to the company

Source: Internet Sales and Marketing Directions, INPUT, 1995, p. 26.

Table 4.1 Primary Reasons for Current Internet Activity

If the potential for increased business dealings is an important reason for the Internet activity, there are a few implications that must be noted. For those functions that need a home base for people and computer to interact with—a site where profit-making companies can make information publicly available—there is the Internet Web site. The Web site facilitates functions such as customer service, marketing, bid solicitation, catalog searching, and order taking. Today, these sites are multiplying at a furious rate. Figure 4.3 shows

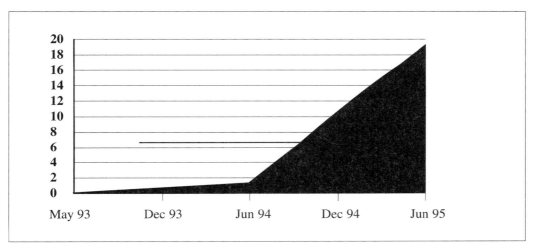

Source: Wanderer (Mathew Gray) and J.P. Morgan Securities Inc., 1995.

Figure 4.3 Number of Public World Wide Web Sites as of June 1995

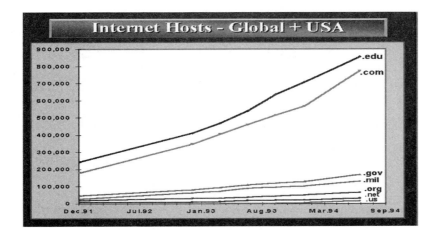

Source: Internet Society.

Figure 4.4 World Wide Web Use as a Percentage of Internet Traffic as of 1994

the number of World Wide Web sites as of June 1995, and Figure 4.4 depicts the global explosion that has been noted in the deployment of the Internet web sites in government, military, commercial, and academic environments.

Many companies are readily embracing Web technologies in the quest for perfect customer service mix, but the costs of achieving the level of excellence provided by the Web sites are high. Table 4.2 shows the comparative cost of establishing and maintaining Web sites of various levels of sophistication.

	COSTS					
	Start-up	**Annual on-going**	**Start-up**	**Annual on-going**	**Start-up**	**Annual on-going**
	LOW	**LOW**	**MEAN**	**MEAN**	**HIGH**	**HIGH**
Sever Hardware	15,000	—	25,000	—	50,000	—
Sever Software	15,000	—	25,000	—	50,000	—
Firewall	10,000	—	12,000	—	25,000	—
Web Content Development	15,000	—	25,000	—	50,000	—
Telecom Links (T1)	10,000	10,000	12,000	12,000	15,000	15,000
Staffing	30,000	30,000	45,000	45,000	50,000	59,000
Hardware Maintenance	2,000	2,000	5,000	5,000	15,000	15,000
Software Maintenance	2,000	2,000	5,000	5,000	10,000	10,000
Content Maintenance	5,000	5,000	10,000	10,000	20,000	20,000
Total Costs	104,000	49,000	164,000	77,000	285,000	110,000

Source: Gartner Group, Inc., Referenced by Daniel Lyons, "Lack of Hard Numbers Fails to Deter Stampede to the Web," *INFOWORLD*, November 5, 1995.

Table 4.2 Cost of Establishing and Maintaining a Web Presence

Advocates say the Web site is the next big advertising frontier; cynics hasten to point out that it's all a fad. However, there is also a common ground—both sides agree that for many companies it's too early to figure out the return they will get on their investment for developing a Web site [3].

In virtually every industry today, CIOs face the challenge of increasing their enterprises' effectiveness by building infrastructures that can be exploited for new market opportunities and leveraging the successes of these infrastructures to open a performance gap between the enterprises and their competitors [4]. In recent months, a few surveys have been conducted by technology research firms such as Forrester Research, Inc., INPUT, International Data Corporation (IDC), and the Gartner Group to understand how people are beginning to view sales and marketing benefits emerging on the newest infrastructure—the Internet. The emerging reports underscore that the most telling comments came from observers who qualify the Internet as the medium that will change the entire marketing paradigm. These observers predict that the future changes will affect how companies do business, with whom, and how the nature of the buyer-seller relationship works. Table 4.3 summarizes the INPUT conducted survey results. Information imperative in terms of advertising, promotion, new distribution channel, and information exchanges of various types dominates the survey results.

MARKETING MIX IMPACTS VISUALIZED	FREQUENCY (%)	EXAMPLES
Promotion	65%	• Information Exchange • Advertising
Place	40	• New Channel • Targeted Selling • Expand Existing Business • Address More People
Price/Product	6	• Less Expensive Marketing • New Product Opportunities
Other	13	• New Sales Paradigm • Market Research

Source: Internet Sales and Marketing Direction, INPUT, 1995, p. 40.

Table 4.3 Areas in Which the Internet Benefits Sales and Marketing

INPUT conducted a survey of forty-eight commercial users of the Internet. The respondents often indicated multiple impacts; thus the percentages are greater than 100 percent.

THE NEW MARKETING PARADIGM

Underlying the INPUT survey results is a scheme that Mammer and Mangurian suggested in *The Changing Value of Communication Technology* [5]. INPUT arranged the various items of the scheme to create a business productivity matrix and presented it to its survey respondents. They were then queried about their perception of the influences and benefits of the Internet. Table 4.4 shows how the respondents measure benefits and where they perceive the Internet actually produces productivity gains. In the range between 1-5, a preference for a 5 indicates that the influence is very important, whereas 1 indicates that

INFLUENCE	BENEFITS TO ORGANIZATION			
	EFFICIENT	EFFECTIVE	INNOVATIVE	COMPOSITE
TIME COMPRESSION	Accelerate Business Process Rating: 3.6	Speed Information Flow Rating: 4.3	Improve Quality Rating: 3.6	Rating 3.9
OVERCOME GEOGRAPHI-CAL LIMITS	Access All Markets Rating: 3.8	Ensure Complete Management Control Rating: 3.1	Penetrate New Markets Rating: 4.0	Rating: 3.6
CHANGE RELATIONSHIPS	Bypass Intermediaries Rating: 3.4	Obtain Scarce Knowledge Rating: 3.6	Build Binding Relationships Rating: 3.7	Rating: 3.6
COMPOSITE	3.6	3.7	3.8	

Source: Internet Sales and Marketing Directions, INPUT, 1995, p. 27

Table 4.4 Perceived Importance of Influences and Benefits of the Internet

it is not important. The importance of influences and benefits from the Internet are perceived to be on the high end, perhaps because the Internet creates a new marketing paradigm: it compresses time, overcomes geographical limitations, and changes customer relations.

Examples such as the eShop Plaza grand opening in early November 1995 on the Internet validates the above respondents' thinking, especially in reference to advertising, targeted selling, expanding existing business, and so forth. eShop Plaza offers convenience and personal service, specials and promotions, and dozens of stores, including Tower Records, 1-800/ FLOWERS, Insight, THE GOOD GUYS!, and Spiegel, that the shoppers can visit for online shopping. With unprecedented full-screen graphics, each store has created its own image and distinct personality [6].

The Tower Records store inside the eShop Plaza has a high-tech appearance and allows the online shopper to browse nineteen different music departments. 1-800/FLOWERS offers a charming online "village" with all kinds of flower arrangements and gift items. Insight, Inc. takes Internet shoppers "inside" a computer to shop for computers, hardware, and software. Thus, each shopping expedition is unique and different.

The various stores in eShop Plaza have been designed and merchandised to showcase their commitment to freshness, unique products, and innovation. Chris McCann, vice president of operations at 1-800/FLOWERS, has plans to transform "traditional" shopping into an easy and feasible online experience. Insight's Manager of Electronic Media, John-Scott Dixon, is equally enthused about the synergies eShop Plaza is creating. Basically, everyone views the eShop's utilization of the state-of-the-art technology as the most convenient and rich shopping experience one can enjoy today and in the future.

THERE IS NO FREE RIDE

The technology of eShop is explicitly connected to overcoming existing business problems and supporting competitive objectives. To further increase consumer benefits, eShop Plaza will use exclusive personal shopping assistants. Their purpose will be to keep track of customers' preferences, make recommendations and steer them toward products and promotions that might interest them. The eShop Plaza merchants are excited about the addition of new "personalities" to the dedicated corps of personal shopping assistants in the months ahead.

The ultimate measure of seriousness about the importance of these types of Internet services may be the investment commitments that eShop and its associated companies are willing to make. The Internet currently carries the perception of an inexpensive marketing vehicle. But the programs that eShop and others are discussing are not free. There is investment for research, development, operations, sales/marketing, and other functions. The Gartner Group, IDC, Forrester Research Group, and INPUT research and survey reports underscore a growing consensus among the consultants: the Internet may be less costly than other alternatives in the long run, but in the short run, *it requires capital. Internet technology is an investment.*

The various investment estimates are based on the best available numbers for accounting, communications, computers, networks, overheads, software, training, and the value of time people spend looking things up. The Gartner Group observes that much of the company expense of acquiring infotech is so deeply buried in several different budget categories that it can never be found [7]. IDC also observes that there are untallied sums spent on in-house development. But the problem is not just the complexity of systems that include interconnected hardware and layers of software. The environment where the new system is implemented varies from company to company, thereby making it difficult for analysts to draw generalizations about the final, itemized bill for Internet technology deployment, maintenance, and utilization.

For first-time planners, the author recommends the Gartner Group's "*How-To Guide.*" [8] It breaks down client/server costs into their component pieces. It also considers factors such as real costs for developing user interfaces and software upgrade costs in the second or third year of implementation. Forrester Research Group also developed a similar

1995			
FUNCTION	MINIMUM	MAXIMUM	AVERAGE
Research	$500	$250,000	$27,000
Development	500	500,000	40,000
Operations	2,000	150,000	28,000
Sales/Marketing	1,000	100,000	20,000
Other	2,000	100,000	30,000
Total	6,000	1,100,000	145,000

Source: Internet Sales and Marketing Directions, INPUT, 1995, p. 30.

Table 4.5 Internet Investment by Functions

client/server cost model based on a study of twenty-five installations [9]. Most of these are pertinent to the Internet deployment issues; these models are useful guides to understanding the simple fact that the economics of client/server or the Internet are situational. INPUT surveyed various companies that are currently involved in developing and implementing technologies for Internet-related activities. Table 4.5 shows the breakdown of the Internet investments by function. The actual development estimate is the largest share of the expenditures. Regardless of the possible variations to be experienced under different company strategies, these are good numbers to start with.

These estimates are the types of information that the CIOs need to produce before the CEOs and CFOs. However, there is one additional twist—the CIOs must also "demonstrate and measure beyond a doubt the value of these types of technology investments." [10]

BETWEEN A ROCK AND A HARD PLACE

In recent times, CIOs have adopted the practice of justifying expenditures by highlighting improvements in productivity, response time, customer complaints, error rates, and nonfiscal measures, rather than measuring the return on investment in information technology through other quantifiable means. CEOs and CFOs, control the purse strings, and they are not entirely sold on the sufficiency of these nonfinancial measures. They want proof that money spent on IT generates earnings and savings that would exceed the investment. CIOs are, therefore, caught between an irresistible force and an immovable object—they are compelled to provide an explanation of IT investment in hard dollars. This is a tall order, because intangible benefits do not readily lend themselves to dollar figures. There lies the challenge: what is needed is a common language for explaining information systems to other executives. If you are a CFO or a CIO, you need to identify and employ techniques for: (a) demonstrating benefits, and, (b) persuasively articulating "soft" benefits wherever possible, in hard dollar terms.

MAKING A CHANGE

The author hopes this part of the book will inspire through example. The Internet is a new phenomenon. In a recent interview, Paul Strassmann, the twenty-first-century consultant and the former Department of Defense CIO, said that he counted over fifty nationally advertised meetings and symposia in the first half of 1995 that were devoted to conjectures on return on the Internet investment [11]. However, any debate about the importance of any new phenomenon becomes less effective unless there is a way to define how to measure it.

During the industrial age, the control of capital was supreme. The crux of all executive decisions was, therefore, the acquisition and investment of capital. The efficiency of using the capital was the accepted measure of corporate performance. Corporations bought equipment based on its *Return-on-Investment*. These corporations paid bonuses on the basis of *Return-on-Assets*. The shares of these corporations were valued by the stock market largely on trends on their *Return-on-Equity*.

Nowadays, it is common to hear that the U.S. has made the transition from an "industrial" to an "information" age. This realization has changed our perception of technology and how it influences our day-to-day performance. Strassmann, after twenty years of experience as a CIO trying to explain budget increases to corporate executives, asserts that the time has come to examine information technology as the essence of most businesses instead of just a machine tool [12]. In "How We Evaluated Productivity"(www.strassmann.com/pubs/eval-productivity.html), he concludes that there is no demonstrable correlation between the financial performance of a firm and the amount it spends on information technologies. An improved method of defining the measurement criteria for return on Internet investment may then very well instigate the nature and extent of investment spending in supporting business missions and contributing to productivity as opposed to the amount being spent. More specifically, you want to review if your company is spending simply for upgrading a particular process or an application, or improving a business function and, through that, integrating your whole enterprise.

In the following examples, we will profile some companies that are upgrading their information infrastructures. Their current practices involve the evaluation of profits with particular reference to the Line of Business Data. These companies reject old justification methods that measure the efficiency of capital, such as return on investment and return on equity. In modern enterprises, capital means less; instead, the performance of high technology and service businesses are influenced by other factors. Hopefully the case materials will allow you to identify these "other factors," and give you greater insight on other ways to define the ROI measurement criteria for information technology. Bear in mind that the Internet is a new phenomenon of information technology. In what follows, your initial focus will to be directed toward the newer business practices for identifying and measuring the "soft" benefits that accrue from information technology development and deployment. This is useful information because the same rationale applies for the Internet situation. Having noted that, it should serve as a good reminder that the review remains partial at best until the type of questions raised on page eighty-four are addressed:

REVIEW

Are these improvements merely to upgrade an existing application, process, or business function?

Do these improvements and measuring techniques help us grasp the nature and extent of benefits accruing from information processing technology deployment?

Do these help us quantify the "soft" benefits in a way that allows us to construct an overall enterprisewide information productivity index?

Are there any better techniques available to address these issues?

A BETTER UNDERSTANDING OF WHERE ROI FALTERS

CogniTech Services Corporation in Easton, Connecticut specializes in measuring the effectiveness of information technology. Their method surveys such subjects as reporting structures, organizational hierarchy, architectures, and corporate and information services cultures to derive a numerical score for their efficiency and effectiveness. The underlying assumption of their method is that effectiveness, not merely efficiency, holds the key to IS success, for "efficiency measures whether a certain activity, product, or service is delivered at the lowest possible cost." Effectiveness, on the other hand, is concerned with the needed results. CogniTech points out that an IS organization could be extremely efficient at developing new applications without being effective [13]. To measure both the effectiveness and efficiency of IS, its approach involves [14]:

1) The identification of key business objectives by department managers

2) The key users' review of IS efforts toward meeting those goals, using four parameters:

  - Actual contribution of IS

  - IS's potential contribution by anticipating needs

  - Importance of IS investments in each unit is compared with other investments

  - Value of IS services compared with their cost

3) The organizational analysis by CogniTech to rate the IS function

4) The determination of IS effectiveness from the above steps

5) The recommendations on how to improve that effectiveness rating

Recently, CogniTech Services Corporation supported Ameritech's efforts to determine its IS effectiveness. Following the steps identified above, it zeroed in on the match between business objectives and technological support for those objectives. It identified key users in five Ameritech operating units and asked them What are their key business objectives for the current fiscal year?

The vice presidents and managers of those units listed their key business objectives for the current fiscal year in the following order:

1) Growing revenues

2) Reducing cycle time

3) Lowering inventory levels

They stated their priorities as exactly and quantitatively as possible. For instance, "15 percent increase in sales" or, for that matter, a "20 percent reduction in inventory" represented a goal.

REVIEW

"IS exists to support the business, enable growth, and help the company discover new opportunities for increased efficiency, productivity, and profitability...IS must give customers what they need, not what we believe they need."

Daniel L. Barth, vice president
IS Division, ClubCorp International [15]

Ameritech's Director of Consulting Services, Eric Christensen, thought that such statements "represented a whole new paradigm for this industry and this company." [16] IS managers now faced a new challenge to enable this type of growth as opposed to just making operations more efficient.

CogniTech, together with the users, rated how IS had helped meet those goals, and based on that exercise, an IS effectiveness rating was arrived at. The results were reviewed by the business and technology managers. Subsequent to that review, there were workshops at each unit to discuss if there were any "gaps" between business needs and IS services. The entire process was time consuming, with a four to six week timetable set for the initial review of several departments in order to get a picture of overall IS effectiveness. This was followed by the follow-up review with a detailed agenda for the workshop at each business unit. There were two positive outcomes: (1) the initial numerical rankings proved to be very helpful; and (2) the workshops clarified the findings of the surveys and helped IS identify immediate actions needed. The survey showed, for instance, that Ameritech did not provide its sales and marketing personnel with easy access to critical customer and market research data. There was a definite need for a synergy between marketing and IS to tap into the records of its massive phone network, and then create a system that could be more effective at providing critical data to marketing groups.

The traditional return on investment calculations do not allow one to identify or quantify these benefits. This is where CogniTech's surveys and workshops reveal the effectiveness of a system. In this example the methodology, taken as a whole, showed that Ameritech's IS culture is "market driven." The business units were happy about a particular warehouse management suite of applications, which involved procurement, purchasing, and warehousing functions. They confirmed the reliability of the system and found the IS managers and staffers to be "extremely well positioned to leverage IS investments within and across departments," and they gave high ratings to Ameritech's IS group [17].

REVIEW

"Thanks to a series of successes over the past few years, IS has earned the right to participate in the strategic business decisions. Senior executives now recognize that IT can help them realize their dreams. When it takes two years to execute a project, those dreams are merely fantasies."

Daniel L. Barth, vice president
IS Division, ClubCorp International [18]

Prior to using CogniTech's methodology, people within Ameritech were often skeptical of IS benefits. But now, the top technologists are routinely involved in high-level strategic decisions that affect the future of the company's business. There is an underlying message in all of this as one tries to grapple with the return on investment decisions: You could be thinking about this shift of attention from information technology to the effectiveness of the executives who manage it. We plan to revisit this point at a later section, but for now, we will review another case from Texas Instruments (TI).

TI is a high-tech manufacturer with $8.5 billion in sales in fiscal year 1993. To maintain its leadership position, TI instituted a formal process to align corporate and technology strategies [19]. An Internal Information Systems Leadership Team, coprised of ten senior managers from TI business units, meets regularly to evaluate proposed and ongoing IS investments. The team approves all strategic IS decisions, subject to a careful review of IS budgets, and progress of major initiatives. The team is essentially TI's "watchdog" committee; the members of the team are there to ascertain if what the technologists are considering will be reasonable to the business. This process achieves better buy-in on both sides. Business units recognize the importance of information technology and, more importantly, IS can make a better determination as to what type of solutions make sense. Any proposal involving significant IS investment is routinely reviewed with all projected hardware, software, services, and personnel costs, plus quantifiable expected benefits. The team also entertains variations of ROI methodology if there is a situation when a project promises largely intangible benefits and the team members must decide if that project is worth pursuing.

Gary Pollard, total quality director for TI's Information Systems and Services group, remembers building a strategic business system for customer order entry, billing, and shipping activities. Its usage encompassed the company's worldwide operations. All items shipped were to be bar coded, and employees in TI warehouses were to scan the contents of each shipment and compare them with the bill of lading. Even though no labor savings resulted from this automation project, the leadership team favored the development and implementation of the system because there would be fewer shipping errors and greater customer satisfaction. Pollard notes the number of shipping errors actually went down to zero. There was no way to project with any certainty the increased revenue that customer satisfaction could generate, but the leadership team rationalized the decision by observing: "our customers would be happier if there were fewer shipping errors."

REVIEW

From a return on investment standpoint, the value of IT in labor savings in the above situation is minimal. The implicit preference is to build follow-on businesses on an existing customer base where initial customer service was enabled by a supporting IT framework, such as automation services. This is the way to determine the value of IT in an enterprise [20].

Besides these watchdog activities, TI information services also initiated a new methodology that called for three stringent "authorization to proceed" reviews before a project could be deployed. Figure 4.5 identifies the checkpoints under each review segment. Again, the team of IS and business unit representatives conducts the reviews.

REVIEW 1 **After "conceptual"** **design**	• Identify project goal and approach • Determine feasibility by IS/business users • Estimate initial cost • Identify expected benefits to customers
REVIEW 2 **After completion of** **application design**	• Determine if project meets user requirements • Review development schedule • Review costs against initial estimates
REVIEW 3 **After completion** **of application** **working prototype**	• Confirm reasonableness of operation costs • Confirm the acceptability of project quality
APPROVAL	• Deploy application in the business

Source: Alice LePlante, "IT's Got What It Takes," *COMPUTERWORLD* October 3, 1994, p. 91.

Figure 4.5 Texas Instruments "Authorization to Proceed" Review Stages

During the first review cycle, IS and the business units involved come to agreement on the project's goal, approach, feasibility, and expected benefits. The flaws become apparent at this stage, but occasionally a proposal would pass through the first review cycle before being canceled. One particular technology investment project was in development for two years. After it reached the second review stage, IS rendered a judgement that the user community would be better served by reengineering their business rather than building an application that was destined to fail. It was not until the design was completed that the TI watchdog committee recognized the futility of this application. The company was going to spend a fortune only to discover that the automation project was severely flawed and would not help solve any problem [21]. This incident validates the claim that this methodology prevents a company from making costly mistakes—"from throwing good money after bad." [22]

THE REAL LANGUAGE OF BUSINESS

The above case histories record two successful methods which Ameritech and TI used to prove the worth of technology investments. They are not identical but there are some common traits: First, the **benefits must be stated in terms that go right to the heart of the company's most important business objectives** such as profitability, increased market share, or customer service to ensure that CEOs and their top managers subscribe to the definition of the value of technology [23]. If the value of technology is defined purely in terms of increasing throughput or improving SQL connectivity etc., CEOs are unlikely to respond to new technology investment proposals. On the other hand, if the technology is described as "enabling a company to cut time to market by three months so it can bludgeon the competition," [24] management will quickly understand and appraise the significance of that kind of an investment option.

To make the case for the Internet technology investment, we can draw parallel conclusions. The traditional ROI methods may not provide any meaningful insight as to whether or not "it really makes sense for us to be out there," remarks Allen Biehl, managing editor of the Novell Web site [25]. However, Marcus Kaufman, director of publications at Novell, refers to the Web site as a necessity. He doesn't know if Novell gets a payback for the dollars it spends on the Web site, but he hastens to add that the Novell Web site receives about 7,000 visitors per hour. For Novell, "the downside risk of not being out there is just too great. So no matter what it cost, we would be out there." [26] To him and many others, benefits come as better customer relations by delivering more information, receiving feedbacks from customers, and responding to them more quickly. Table 4.6 summarizes the findings of a recent survey of sixty-four respondents on the importance of potential Internet benefits. Respondents were asked to rank order their perceptions in the range between 1-5, with 5 being "Very Important" and 1 "Not Important." The overall perception is that customer relations is the most important Internet benefit.

Secondly, some benefits defy quantification and it is common knowledge that the IS profession values precision. Financial experts and marketing number-crunchers value numeric measures. The challenge is to find a common ground where both sides have ample scope for (a) giving consideration to "soft" benefits; and (b) measuring and analyzing benefits that are meaningful to general management in terms of profitability of the enterprise. It is a deadly serious exercise, but if properly done according to a technique described in

POTENTIAL INTERNET BENEFIT	CONSOLIDATED RATING
Delivering more information	4.4
Receiving feedback from customers	4.3
Enhancing relationship with customers	4.2
Responding more quickly to customers	4.2
Delivering sales information less expensively	4.1
Promoting products through new media	4.1
Adding new sales channels	4.0
Providing better sales information	4.0
Obtaining new customers	4.0
Supporting customers less expensively	3.8
Targeting individuals	3.8
Testing new sales strategies	3.6

Source: Internet Sales and Marketing Directions, INPUT, 1995, p. 41.

Table 4.6 Ratings of Importance of Potential Internet Benefits

the following section, it is possible to derive numbers that could make an honest but convincing argument.

A RESOUNDING MAYBE

The leadership team at TI and also Marcus Kaufman at Novell decided, as outlined in the preceding section, in favor of the Internet deployment despite the uncertainty concerning immediate returns on investment. Their position statements underscore that in today's economy, businesses are becoming profitable because of their *Management* and not because of capital.

Return On Investment (ROI) and other justification methods have a project authorization bias. They critically review capital budgeting with the intention of exercising maximum influence over future directions of a business. Once a capital investment gets approved, the operating expenses follow from the initial investment decision. The annual costs are fixed; no major changes are possible. The management attempts to estimate expected benefits and costs for all innovation with reasonable confidence. If this investment-oriented logic is applied to system automation or infrastructure development, it will invariably favor projects that automate existing business procedures instead of changing them to take advantage of the new information-handling methods. In this framework, emphasis tends to be on controlling new investments as evidenced in the case histories. In many instances, this tendency has led to the identification and establishment of the information system as a *discrete and separate function*, and resulted in misapplications of technology because goals and actions got confused. Coming up with proof that the desired goals have been reached is a tough assignment, especially if a proposed technology project requires unanimous approval from constituencies who have conflicting requirements, opposing interests, and diverse qualifications in considering the merits of the project. Unless there is a measurable financial outcome for an information technology project, the clarity of its goal is questionable. When the Internet is introduced into an organization, its effects will to be systemic, affecting the working of the whole enterprise. The consequences will modify the way the enterprise conducts its business. In view of this, measurements must record the aftereffects of many changes, instead of just one isolated improvement. This raises a pertinent issue: How do you set the goals for the Internet technology investments? What principles help you evaluate a scheme for changing systems that manage an organization?

The answer is: You should measure *productivity* of your enterprise before and after the Internet deployment. If you see gains in organizational productivity, you know that the Internet improved overall performance. If yours is an information-based enterprise, your rational choice would be to integrate the information system into every manager's job, and measure "management productivity" instead of "capital" or "labor productivity." ROI fails to show that the performance of high technology and service businesses are influenced more by the quality of their management than by their assets. It can no longer explain why companies in equivalent markets, with similar capital structure, and with the same information infrastructures, deliver remarkably different financial results.

But in today's dynamic environment, you as a CEO or CFO need to extract business value from your investments in the Internet technology. You need a methodology that shows more clearly how to determine the economic profit or economic value added (EVA) [27], as it is being defined today. You want to show the shareholders how many dollars of net gain accrue to them [the shareholders] for every dollar paid for management. Bearing these points in mind, a methodology based on the concept of *Return-on-Management*

(R-O-M) is presented here. The ratio is derived by first isolating the *Management Value-added* of an enterprise, and then dividing it by the enterprise's total *Management Costs.* To estimate the cost of management, the expenses of sales, general & administrative (S.G.&A) and research & development (R&D), as reported in published financial statements, are added. The basis for this estimation method is discussed in the forthcoming book *Alignment of Information Management.* (The Information Economics Press, 1996 [28].)

Management Value-added is what remains after every contributor to an enterprise's inputs gets paid. If *Management Value-added* is greater than *Management Costs*, we can justifiably say that managerial efforts are productive because the managerial *outputs* exceed managerial *inputs* [29]. Figure 4.7 illustrates the cost elements for deriving the *Management Value-added.*

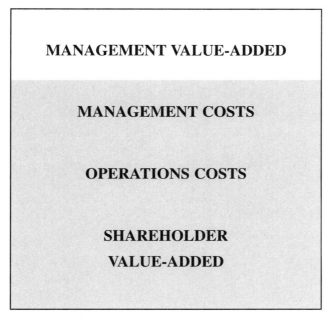

Source: Paul A. Strassmann, "Introduction to ROM Analysis: Linking Management Productivity and Information Technology," Strassmann.com/consulting/ROM-intro/Intro_to_ROM.html, p. 11.

Figure 4.7 Cost Elements for Deriving the Management Value-added

R-O-M(TM) Index is therefore a function of **Management Output** and **Management Input** and it gives **Management Productivity** [30]. Unlike the other techniques we have reviewed, it identifies productivity of the enterprises, regardless of their size, the number of client/servers they have installed, or how many systems professionals they employ. It has been empirically verified that R-O-M is the only statistic that shows a positive relationship to IT spending [31].

Paul Strassmann examined the 1995 *COMPUTERWORLD* (CW) Premier 100 companies, which ranked corporations by *Information Productivity* and compared them against the top Fortune 100 corporations, ranked by *revenue*. He documented that for the period from 1992 through 1994, the CW Premier 100 companies delivered 347 percent more sales growth, 334 percent more growth in shareholder equity and 46.2 percent more employment growth, when compared with the big 100 corporations. (See Table 4.7). To develop the listing of the CW Premier 100 companies, Strassmann ranked 5,000 U.S. corporations by *Information Productivity* (Refer to Appendix A).

CW Premier 100 Companies			Fortune 100 Companies		
	1992	**1994**	**Growth**	**1992**	**1994**	**Growth**
Net Sales	65,152,154	92,086,506	41.3%	1,938,707,606	2,169,627,321	11.9%
Shareholder Equity	36,522,568	56,868,252	55.7%	628,033,046	732,696,463	16.7%
Sales, Gen & Admin	11,809,902	13,707,939	16.1%	497,963,151	520,523,106	4.53%
Research & Development	2,901,620	3,778,062	30.2%	25,239,650	22,986,013	-8.9%
Employment	566,157	828,003	46.2%	9,710,166	9,614,949	-1%

Source: Paul A. Strassmann, "Productivity, not Bigness, Is Beautiful," *COMPUTERWORLD*, September 19, 1995.

Table 4.7 Information Productivity(TM) Rankings, Industrial Companies

R-O-M(TM) Productivity Index relates to the numbers that are watched and understood **by the board of directors, top executives, and shareholders** and offers a sound basis from which to start discussions on how to do better in the future. The Index is highly suitable for analyzing major investment proposals involving information technologies. This point is further explained below.

Information (e.g., Management) assures survival of a firm in a competitive environment. Without continuous intervention by Management, every enterprise will perish from chaotic conditions which arise when external information (about customers and competitors) and internal information fails to guide people in what to do. Through the case materials, we have already verified and validated the need for Management intervention. The critical task at hand now is to determine how much information (Management) is necessary to run an enterprise. Earlier we had an implicit reference to this issue and you were asked to think about it. It may have become clear that central to the issue of Management is the generation of a positive Net Value-added in order to survive. A corporation becomes profitable only when it generates a net surplus of wealth. For auditing purposes, traditionally the corporation would evaluate annually: [1]

GROSS RETURN based on:

1) Additional revenue per year

2) Direct savings per year
    — One-time savings
    — Annual savings

3) Productivity
    — Savings from processing more
      information electronically annually

4) Indirect savings
    — Annual savings resulting from the avoidance of additional
      staffing, etc.

First year total Return On Investment: $$$

Subsequent total annual ROI: $$$

COSTS

Hardware and software costs

---

[1] The author gratefully acknowledges Richard Pastore, Frank Giege,r and The Gartner Group's ideas on various management strategies to control cost [32].

— Operating System costs
— Administration costs:
— Support costs:
— Application costs
— Administration costs:
— Support costs:

One time training costs:

First year total enterprise costs:

Subsequent total annual costs:

First year net ROI: $$$

Subsequent net annual ROI: $$$

It is crucial is to review and understand that *Management* has the capacity to develop an organization that extracts from the hostile environment *Net Value-added (Outputs)* in excess of total costs *(Inputs)*. Management of information is inseparable from management's general roles. **The processing of information by Internet can and should, therefore, be viewed as an extension of traditional management roles, by other means.**

The empirical evidence suggests that the R-O-M Productivity Index is a technique that could add value to investment analysis concerning Internet technology development and implementation. It is the only methodology that opens the door to exploring, measuring, and quantifying the "soft" benefits of the Internet technology by its principal customers— the managers of the enterprise information. The old ROI formulation can now be replaced by directly measuring the productivity of Management as an information-processing function. To that end, there are some analytical advantages you can derive immediately. The use of the Internet services and applications will not be evenly distributed among workers in your enterprise. The value-added option in the R-O-M technique will allow your enterprise to get a better understanding of the Internet's effectiveness by separating its managerial uses from other applications. Your enterprise can then evaluate the effectiveness of Management with or without the Internet services. Additionally, your enterprise can isolate cases showing superior managerial productivity, and then examine the characteristics of the Internet use that differ from cases that show inferior managerial productivity.

CogniTech's approach, as outlined earlier, was to identify business objectives by department managers. A further refinement to that approach is to extract the perspectives of management at levels differentiated by:

1) Officials

2) Managers

3) Professionals

4) Technicians

5) Skilled workers

6) Unskilled workers

Your mission is to conduct an annual audit for your enterprise, including whole company as well as operating divisions. You, as decision makers, want the users' views on IS efforts to justify the importance of Internet investments in each unit compared with other investments. You want them to articulate:

1) What percent of the enterprise devices resident in each respondent's division or unit has access to the Internet E-Mail or other Internet services, facilities, and tools?;

2) How much does the enterprise gain in the way of productivity by spending on Internet not included in explicit budget items such as hardware, software, data and voice communications, supplies, and outside vendor support, etc.?

You should insist that these questions be part of a larger checklist for a complete professional survey to be conducted by a competent outside research firm to be objective. Further, by reviewing such financial data should be reviewed:

- Net Sales

- Sales and General Administrative Expense

- Research and Development Expense

- Profit after Taxes

- Shareholder Equity, etc.

The firm will add value to the survey by benchmarking your company's usage of the Internet against the other companies in the industry. These details will provide better facts and figures on the management productivity improvement due to Internet deployment. (Refer to Appendix A: 1993 Information Productivity Rankings, Industrial Companies.) Armed with such foresight, you, as decision makers, can make better Internet investment plans for the future.

Chapter **5**

Internet Policy for the Enterprise

"Enterprises need to codify their practices and procedures to protect their data and IS resources from hostile networking environments, and to effectively use the Internet."

Gartner Group
Conference Presentation
March 1995.

PUT IT IN WRITING

The concluding remarks of the last chapter suggested that there could be superior and inferior managerial productivity based on the Internet use. To clarify "inferior productivity," the Internet is still going through its adolescence and has much maturing to do. Current efforts are concentrated in developing tools and finding and structuring interesting sets of information and data to view with the tools. As exciting and productive as these developments are, therein also lies the cause of concern for enterprises. While using the tools, employers may make inadvertent mistakes or deliberately mishandle information on the Internet. If and when that happens, the enterprise may face problems ranging from embarrassment, employer liability, and copyright violations, to loss of trade secrets, loss of productivity, or information overload [1].

During the Third Annual Ernst & Young/InformationWeek Information Security Survey, twenty companies reported information security losses in excess of $1 million. The Internet business users that exchange information externally reported numerous successful or attempted break-ins in the past year. According to the Federal Bureau of Investigation, 80 percent of all computer crimes reported to the agency involve the use of Internet to break into computer systems [2]. Most companies express concern that they do not have proper tools, well trained personnel, or properly developed guidelines and/or policies to protect the enterprises from information [security] losses. But most of the Ernst & Young survey respondents demonstrated "growing awareness of security problems and increased willingness to devote additional resources to their solution." [3] A commanding 87 percent of Internet users stated that they would use the Internet more for business purposes if they could devise a good workable policy for security and maintenance of a productive workplace. They all agreed that as companies rely on the Internet to exchange data among remote locations, effective guidelines will be needed that could be centrally developed and uniformly enforced at all locations of an enterprise. These guidelines should address the Internet features that must be monitored for developing policy on access, use, and disclosure of information through the Internet.

Hypermedia presentation is an operational feature that needs careful monitoring. The presentation should be highly representative and descriptive of the enterprise's work. It is important to reflect an accurate, overall picture of the enterprise and guard against the possibility of letting anyone produce and publish anything that is piecemeal, misleading, or incomplete [4]. There is a preference here for management approval and authorization of the content of enterprise information for Internet use. Management approval and authorization is an enforcement issue that deals primarily with rules governing a particular type of information. Agreement on rules is best arrived at by negotiation with those most knowledgeable about particular data and information and how they should be structured and presented in an online, hypermedia environment. The details need to be developed by the joint efforts of many people from different sources within an enterprise. The origin and control of information content might very well be at the enterprise's grass roots level. If a mechanism is put in place that brings all the relevant [technical] people together, the rules concerning security, authentication, link management, markup language standards, etc. could be properly developed, updated on a regular basis, and satisfactorily applied toward drafting and interpreting an enterprisewide Internet policy. The mechanism is beneficial to the policy process in that it is more likely to produce a policy consistent with the enterprise's business goals and strategies. It will involve successful collaboration among executives from IS, security, human resources, legal, marketing, pricing, advertising, customer relations, government affairs, purchasing, research, and operations. This involvement will have a far reaching impact on decisions regarding the policy to be adopted. The different representatives will be able to articulate their individual and collective experiences in controlling and decontrolling access to external/internal information and managing advertising, promotion, marketing, and electronic commerce-related Internet transmissions. Collective awareness will facilitate a clear, wise, and sophisticated understanding of the issues that will produce a "workable" strategy document.

CAUTION

"You can't just put equipment out there and let people use it for illegal purposes [5]."

Attorney Helena Kobrin

Once the policy is baselined, it should be distributed to all layers of management within an enterprise. It will inform everybody what needs to be done to reduce security losses, including disciplinary actions that must be taken in case of policy violations. It will also have a substantial impact on advising management that personal authority and accountability matters most in presenting the enterprise and its activities appropriately to the public. When the policy document promulgates professional standards of conduct, it is likely to spur creative individual use of the Internet resources, while furnishing guidelines for the most appropriate, efficient, and safe usage of Internet resources.

ENTERPRISE FUNCTIONS AND SUGGESTED POLICIES

Chapter 3 includes a sample home page for an airline. As Figure 3.1 illustrates, a typical home page contains general information, facts and figures, news items about the company, a disclaimer, and several links to other company literature. This home page is the company's own proprietary document. As such, what goes on behind the scene to create, manage, review, modify, and change with a view to keeping the page current, should be handled carefully, seriously, and with a sense of urgency. More specifically, there are three **tactical** problems that the CEOs/CFOs/CIOs must address: how to get a handle on what goes on over the Internet, how to identify the risks, and how to minimize the legal and management costs of doing business on the Internet. Additionally, the CIO often has a strategic challenge of being a "visionary" toward the tasks of aligning business and technology goals and implementing sound enterprise Internet policies.

Enterprise strategies are those practices that result in "guidelines and policies" that impact how Internet use and support processes are conducted. Table 5.1 provides a high-level breakdown of management strategies that reflect a philosophy and methodology based on extensive experience in addressing enterprisewide Internet issues [6]. It begins with a listing of the component functions associated with the purpose of the enterprise's Internet project. The core strategies, if implemented, will provide an opportunity for an enterprise to achieve a collaborative relationship among the various divisions and also maintain bottom line Internet objectives of service quality, customer satisfaction, risk management, and legal cost control. Based on this outline, Acceptable Use Policy (AUP) framework [8], and reviews of several other interim guidelines prepared by such agencies as the National Institute of Standards and Technology, an illustrative example of Internet policy is presented here. The hypothetical company is RB Enterprises. This is a starting place for developing a coherent policy on Enterprise Internet use. It should be viewed as a useful resource, but not the final authority. Different enterprises will have different resources and rules and this piece *cannot* cover every enterprise and its various jurisdictions. Instead, the purpose here is to define a lasting statement of what an enterprise's intent is toward the Internet [8]. Further, the audience for this work is comprised of decision makers (CEOs/CFOs/CIOs) and, in this instance, middle management and system administrators. This work is not directed at engineers or programmers who are trying to deploy the Internet with secure programs. Rather, the focus here is on policies and procedures that must be in place to support the Internet services that an enterprise may be implementing.

An important feature for policy making is a long-term look at Internet use—what will be the enterprise's relation to the Internet in five or fifteen years? A broad policy statement will allow the enterprise to keep the original policy statement unchanged for a reasonably long period, but its implementation will always be subject to change. For instance, a broad policy statement articulates what is acceptable and unacceptable use of the Internet. At extreme ends, it is fairly clear what the issues are, but issues at the center are harder to define. For example, at what point is sending E-Mail by Internet to a friend too far from

Internet: Management Strategies

Purpose of the Enterprise Internet Project
Marketing on the Internet
Selling on the Internet
Facilitating markets on the Internet
Disseminating information on the Internet
◆
Effective and Efficient Usage
Mandatory training requirements
Moderating/Monitoring/Participating in USENET/Electronic discussion groups
Qualifications for access authority
Handling "advertising," lead generation
Professional standards in posts—disclaimers
Web pages must professionally represent enterprise
◆
Classes of Mail Allowed
Casual Communications
"Official Correspondence"
◆
Restrictions on Nonprofessional Usage
Inappropriate humor, graphics/images, chain letters
◆
Protecting Proprietary Information
Proprietary information sharing restrictions
Uploading/downloading copyrighted materials
◆
Security Awareness
"Rogue" and "back door" Internet connections
Firewall policies
◆
Virus Awareness
Risks of downloads
Problems of virus scanning
◆
Support Resources
Who authorizes usage
Who maintains Web presence
◆
Disciplinary Actions for Policy Violations
◆
Policy Review Committee Representatives
◆
Appendix: Netiquette Tutorial
◆
Inclusions by Reference: Corporate E-Mail and Security Policies

Table 5.1 Enterprise Internet Policy Outline

being acceptable? Those gray areas are left to the discretion of the key enterprise executives.

As the Internet practices grow and officials are assured that the enterprise's reputation, proprietary information, software or similar other interests are not being compromised, some concessions for private E-Mail use or similar uses may be made. The productivity/Internet relationship is always going to be a major concern for the enterprises [9]. It is incumbent upon each enterprise to put any area off limits and that essentially is the implementation strategy angle that the senior management, HR, legal counsel, employee users, security, union representatives, the MIS director, and the CIO of an enterprise must tackle. If the illustrative material aids in the actual development of an Internet Implementation Policy, this section of the book will have served its purpose.

RB ENTERPRISES'S INTERNET POLICY DIRECTIVE

Purpose of the Enterprise Internet Project

This term Internet refers to the World Wide Web (WWW), bulletin boards, anonymous file transfer protocol (FTP) the and other services. Much has been written lately about the Internet, its components, and the emerging commercial advantages these services and features offer. With all this attention, it is important to evaluate the potential of the Internet and seize the opportunity to exploit its commercial advantages. Since the Internet provides access across a number of interconnected networks, information on a server directly connected to the Internet is available to everyone on the Internet. Information that is placed on the Internet must, therefore, be cleared through appropriate channels as other publicly released material.

The purpose of the Enterprise Internet project is to develop a policy for using the Internet as a transmission media to distribute information both inside and outside the enterprise. The following is released as an Interim Policy and remains in effect until superseded by a formal fully coordinated Enterprise Internet Policy. This Interim Policy acknowledges the complex and explosive growth of the Internet technology which the company plans to leverage with the initial focus being given to the following areas. [10]

A. *Marketing on the Internet*

The company will authorize marketing activities over the Internet, subject to appropriate coordination and supervision by the respective department heads. These activities will take any of several forms.

First, the Internet will be used as a medium for advertising. Interactive sales-related marketing information will be provided over the Internet, especially for big-ticket items, so that the consumers get as much information as possible before committing to a purchase.

Secondly, the company will leverage the interactivity and multilayered nature of a Web site to learn about the different information accessed by different groups of online consumers and recycle this information back into the future marketing efforts.

Also, the company will market to commercial accounts over the Internet. It will distribute technical product information including technical specification and a host of related product data to commercial customers, subject to appropriate departmental authorization.

B. Selling on the Internet

The company will offer goods through online catalogs, use electronic order forms, and furnish shipping and credit card information while online.

The company will make sales to commercial accounts over the Internet. It will use the Internet to exchange information such as bidding documents and sales orders with the suppliers, subject to supervision and approval by the supervisory and management staff of the appropriate department.

C. Facilitating Markets on the Internet

The company will leverage the various Internet facilities: "smart agents," virtual mall, and Internet directories. In the business-to-business context, the company will use private procurement systems to establish links to proprietary computer networks as business warrants expansion along those lines.

D. Disseminating Information on the Internet

As noted under section A, the company will provide information on the Internet, under supervision and control of senior management, to enable consumers make better informed purchasing decisions.

Effective and Efficient Use

This section promulgates Internet usage policy guidance to satisfy new and changing legal and management issues.

Mandatory Training Requirements

The law regarding the intersection of legal issues and Internet technology is emerging, but as the company plans to leverage the Internet for commercial gains, it must minimize its potential legal exposure [11].

The company shall mandate that all employees undergo training on Internet productivity and etiquette.

The corporate training department will coordinate training schedules with the other line of business units.

The training will be updated and repeated as often as is deemed necessary by the supervisory and management staff.

For the benefit of all employees, the training will be comprehensive.

It will instruct the employees about the restrictions that apply for Internet E-Mail, games, or browsing for personal reasons.

It will instruct the employees about the company's risk of defamation claims and provide necessary guidelines for employees who have specific business to conduct in chat channels and bulletin boards.

It will instruct employees about the prohibition of and ramifications for unauthorized use of the Internet or bulletin boards, sharing of confidential passwords, or downloading and installing software.

Upon satisfactory conclusion of the training, each employee shall sign and return an employee agreement and corporate Internet policy to the respective department manager for his/her cognizance. The manager will submit that to HR for record keeping.

Moderating/Monitoring/Participating in Electronic Discussion/USENET Groups

To avoid facing liability, RB Enterprises expressly prohibits all employees and/or third parties from using Internet system with an account bearing the enterprise ".com" domain name to moderate, monitor, or participate in moderated or unmoderated bulletin boards ("BBS"), listservs, chat groups, forums, or other "online cocktail parties."

If and when special needs arise, the respective supervisory personnel and department managers will review and approve individual participation requests on a case by case basis.

RB Enterprises mandates the use of the following outbound E-Mail and discussion disclaimers:

"This message represents the personal views and opinions of the individual sender and should in no way be construed as an authorized communication on behalf of RB Enterprises [12]."

Qualifications for Access Authority

RB Enterprises's staff will be authorized to fully use the Internet services and facilities, where feasible, as a mechanism for making enterprise-acquired data resources broadly available to the public. However, all employees must adhere to the administrative policies and procedures that have been devised for Internet services, including limitations on the use of the Internet for those activities that support RB Enterprises's business missions.

RB Enterprises reserves the right to monitor, review, and regulate usage of the Internet and any of its services to ensure that the enterprise policy is followed, services are used purely for business purposes, and RB Enterprises's rights are protected.

The employees are responsible for keeping their access codes and passwords. The employees shall never give out the access codes and passwords to anybody. If anyone asks for an employee's access code and/or password, the employee must refuse and report the incident to the IS department.

Only the director of the IS and the legal department shall have access to all employee access codes and passwords. They will have the authority to revoke a user's access code and password in the event of a perceived danger to the continued operation of a system, its integrity, or risk to the user community.

Handling "Advertising," Lead Generation

RB Enterprises will use the Internet as another medium for advertising. It will exhibit caution because there are virtually no restrictions on the amount of information transmitted and the feedback that can be received via the Internet [13].

While advertising on the Internet, RB Enterprises shall use particular care about the information being disseminated. The traditional legal risks of advertising, namely copyright and trademark infringement, deceptive practices, consumer protection, defamation, privacy, publicity, and trade or product disparagement are also in effect in the Internet medium.

Additionally, if RB Enterprises provides "hyperlinks" in its online advertising, which will allow the user to go from one page to a totally independent page containing actionable (e.g., false, defamatory, deceptive) content on the jumped-to page, it increases RB Enterprises's legal exposure. As RB Enterprises turns to the Internet—more specifically, to the World Wide Web—to advertise, all advertising materials shall be cleared through the respective department's supervisory and management staff before being placed on the Internet.

Under authority of RB Enterprises's supervisory and management staff, the enterprise will post product information in the form of text, pictures, and interactive activities including short movies, if and when such advertising adds value to the campaign.

RB Enterprises will track the frequency and manner in which different consumers navigate through the information and thus gather data for future marketing campaigns.

Professional Standards in Posts—Disclaimers

Refer to the example under subsection Moderating/Monitoring/PSarticipating in Electronic Discussion/USENET Groups.

Web pages must professionally represent enterprise

RB Enterprises' public face is its Web page(s) and it mandates that management shall ensure that the published information on the Web page(s) is up to date, consistent, accurate, and properly integrated with other referenced materials, including audio and video. It further mandates the management to institute a procedure for regular continual review of the enterprise's Web page(s) for quality and accuracy.

RB Enterprises will invest in the Web to disseminate information deemed useful by the public. Accordingly, its policy states that all employees will have collective responsibility for quality control of the material the enterprise publishes. It further instructs that as employees develop good representative literature on the enterprise and its products and services, they shall adhere to the house styles.

Management will create an Enterprise-level System Administration (WebMaster) function which will:

1) oversee information on the RB Enterprises's WWW Internet in coordination with other senior executives;

2) provide organizational structure guidance for all RB Enterprises's WWW Internet pages;

3) review and validate RB Enterprises' WWW Internet requirements to add features and services to the Internet system;

4) maintain an RB Enterprise WWW House Style Guidelines document or set of documents;

5) provide oversight of the RB Enterprises's Guidelines Document.

RB Enterprises management will create an Organizational-level System Administration (WebMaster) function which will:

1) address overall management of the Organizational/Functional Pages and/or Server;

2) address management of the information on the RB Enterprises's server, directory, or pages;

3) address configuration management and system integrity for the RB Enterprises' Internet pages;

4) Review and validate the organizational/functional Internet requirements with the RB Enterprises's WebMaster to add features and services requested to be placed on the RB Enterprises's WWW Internet system;

5) ensure that the organizational/functional information is current, consistent, and valid;

6) check to verify that the links are operational and all outages are corrected;

7) advise RB Enterprises's WebMaster on advanced planning for further development, enhancements, or upgrades.

Classes of Mail Allowed

RB Enterprises will use the Internet to keep departments, work groups, and individuals in close contact. It recognizes that E-Mail is the primary way that people on the Internet communicate with each other. It acknowledges that many people become more communicative because they prefer sending E-Mail to talking on the phone or sending letters by U.S. postal service. RB Enterprises's E-Mail policy is that the enterprise will use E-Mail to convey direct messages that can be answered quickly and pertain to a specific workplace task. It is not just another way to talk to someone. To define the entire scope of this E-Mail policy, RB Enterprises makes specific references to:

Casual Communications

E-Mail is not conversation and it does not convey emotion well, but it is recorded and can easily be duplicated [14]. While E-Mail may be less formal than a hard copy letter, it is more permanent than speaking to someone on the phone. In the event of a litigation, it may be subject to discovery. Employees should take this possibility under advisement when sending E-Mail both within and outside of the company. RB Enterprises's guidelines in this matter are:

1) Formulate your message correctly.

2) Use telephone when appropriate.

3) Use separate bulletin boards so people do not interfere with other people's work [15].

4) Do not use E-Mail for unrelated advertising.

5) Do not use E-Mail for casual communications concerning events such as golf tournaments, garage sales, girl scout cookies, fund raisers, or "puppies for sale."[16]

Official Correspondence

Internal or external E-Mail messages shall be treated as business records. RB Enterprises requires that all employees practice good record keeping. This will protect the employees in terms of their ability to prove the contents of a communication or that the information was actually sent or received, should the need arise.

1) The Records Retention Policy that is in place for paper filing applies to business E-Mail in terms of how long the records should be protect-

ed and when these could be destroyed; therefore, all employees shall file business E-Mail either electronically or print and place them in the paper files.

2) All employees shall keep these files organized and up to date at all times.

3) Employees shall not send courtesy copies of an E-Mail message to people, unless these people have a need to view a particular message.

4) Employees shall not forward E-Mail messages unless the original sender knows that the message may be forwarded.

5) Employees are not required to acknowledge an E-Mail just to inform the sender that they have received it.

6) RB Enterprises's line managers who notice excessive charges for their group's E-Mail account shall be authorized to request a detailed account of all E-Mail transactions to ascertain who is sending messages to whom.

7) RB Enterprises reserves rights to monitor and review E-Mail messages to ensure that the employees are adhering to the enterprise policy and to revise the existing policy guidelines regarding use and the potential risks and consequences of misuse of E-Mail services.

Restrictions on Nonprofessional Usage

A variety of communication icons have evolved to express humor, sarcasm, surprise, anger, or bewilderment and these have found popular use on the Internet. Some of these have been developed so that the reader will better understand the intent and context of the message, rather than taking it the wrong way. There are also some abbreviations that are supposed to be commonly understood. Notwithstanding the cautions and clues people ascribe to the unique character of the Internet, RB Enterprises takes the position that every transmission over a computer network is potentially a communication of sort. A communication could be defamatory if someone claims it has adversely affected his or her reputation. Some forms of communication are considered so injurious by nature that proof of damages will not be required. For the protection of all employees and its own interests, RB Enterprises shall be governed by the following guidelines.

Inappropriate Humor, Graphics/Images, Chain letters

The Internet links many different communities with many different standards. In the eye of the law, when one set of standards that is acceptable for one community is sent by computer transmission into another community that is guided by another set of standards, the recipient community's standards prevail. As Internet users, RB Enterprises's employees must always be mindful of how their words may be interpreted and how they may be held liable for inappropriate humor, graphics/images, and/or chain letters. As such, they shall refrain from:

1) sending, displaying, or printing sexually explicit or suggestive images;

2) using objectionable language in both public and private messages;

3) sending chain letters that could cause congestion and disruption of networks and systems.

Protecting Proprietary Information

RB Enterprises equates the Internet with "public access." Its policy is that transmitting or providing access to company proprietary technical data over the Internet is tantamount to unauthorized disclosure. Such data will reveal information in violation of contractual obligations or release product details that prematurely affect the company's stock price.

Further, the policy states that no employees should transmit any unencrypted, company confidential technical information over the Internet unless it has been approved by cognizant management staff for public release by attaching appropriate distribution statement(s). Access to databases containing restricted data should not be granted over the Internet. To ensure that the employees clearly understand and adhere to these policies, the following procedural guidelines shall remain in effect until further notice.

Proprietary Information Sharing Restrictions

RB Enterprises shall release information to the public through the Internet only as necessary to safeguard information requiring protection in accordance with its established business programs, strategies, and goals. Its management shall implement the provisions of this policy by:

1) Issuing instructions for the internal administration/enforcement of the requirements prescribed herein.

2) Forwarding information proposed for release over the Internet to appropriate supervisory and management personnel for clearance and including specific recommendations concerning the material being submitted for review and concurrence.

Uploading/Downloading Copyrighted Materials

RB Enterprises will engage in digitizing its products and services to allow consumers to download the contents of their desired purchase(s) directly from the Internet. It is cognizant of the fact that the law is undeveloped in the matter of online distribution of digitized products [17].

As RB Enterprises plans the future distribution of demos, updates, patches, and, in certain cases, full product over the Internet, it mandates that all employees become familiar with the potential antitrust and unfair competition claims, franchise questions, and other distribution laws involving copyright, patent, and trademark issues. Also, before placing any of its digitized products for online distribution, RB Enterprises must meet all provisions of the United States export laws. To avoid any possibility of wrongdoing in above matters, any RB Enterprises's employees transmitting or receiving products online must adhere to the following directives:

Uploading software

1) Review licensing and intellectual property policies prior to making software universally available

2) Seek RB Enterprises's supervisory and management personnel and legal affairs' concurrence and approval in ascertaining the scope of potential audience as well as particular laws of jurisdictions in which software will be made available

Downloading software

1) Seek RB Enterprises's supervisory and management personnel and legal affairs concurrence and approval in ascertaining licensing and intellectual property restrictions on use or dissemination of product, if any

Security Awareness

RB Enterprises recognizes the vulnerability of existing security software and will use every precaution necessary to safeguard its confidential information before placing it on the Internet.

This section does not address how to design or implement secure systems or programs. Rather, the focus here is on policies and procedures that need to be developed to support the technical security features. This section is addressed to the enterprise management, and promulgates the following policy guidance to satisfy changing Internet-related security concerns [18]:

1) Information to be protected

2) Threats to information security

3) Likelihood of threats

4) Measures that will protect the enterprise's assets in a cost-effective manner

5) Continual process review and improvement

Enterprise management shall pay close attention to items 4 and 5, while monitoring:

Firewall Policies

Management will decide what firewall mechanism is appropriate: blocking traffic or permitting traffic. The fundamental concern of RB Enterprises's firewall policies is to protect against unauthenticated interactive logins from the "outside" world.

"Rogue" and "Back Door" Internet Connections

RB Enterprises recognizes that firewalls cannot protect against attacks that do not go through the firewall. It is concerned that a "helpful" employee might inadvertently end up giving modem pool access to an attacker. If and when that happens, the attacker will be able to break into the enterprise's network by completely bypassing the firewall and leak company proprietary data through that route.

RB Enterprises's management will ensure that Internet connections have a coherent policy about how dial-up access via modems should be protected. Management shall make the firewall a part of a consistent overall organizational security architecture and guard against the possibility of users independently establishing back door modem accounts which could put the enterprise at risk [19].

Reporting Security Problems

RB Enterprises will facilitate training of its employees to ensure protection of its computer resources from hackers who deliberately penetrate various enterprise systems from the Internet to damage the systems and databases. All employees must adhere to the procedures enunciated in these training sessions.

The employees will address problems and report suspected misuse of their accounts or other misuse they may notice through the company's electronic mail address ("security"). If they feel an immediate need to establish direct personal contact with an appropriate authority, they may approach the system administrator who manages Internet security.

The system administrator shall post warnings about security breaches and also issue immediate solutions and software patches to problems as they are discovered. The system administrator will further investigate the suspicious activities and maintain a log of the investigation, actions, and findings.

If the system administrator decides it is necessary to examine files belonging to a user, he or she will advise other senior management as necessary to ensure that the individual rights are not violated, and that the facilities, services, and data for which the system administrator is responsible are protected.

Virus Awareness

A virus attack is not immediately evident in most organizational settings. RB Enterprises understands that the initial infection can go unseen for months and by the time the problem is identified, the damage may be widespread.

To prevent virus attacks, RB Enterprises shall maintain a strong and enforced company policy against any illegal software. The Enterprise systems administrator will keep the employees informed about the distinction between normal control structures and viruses, and set up controls to trap and eliminate computer viruses.

RB Enterprises is fully aware that viruses are brought in by contact with infected disks, or by local programming. Trojan Horses are crude, front door attacks, and they can be inadvertently introduced via a network, or on a disk. Accordingly, RB Enterprises mandates the system administrator to specifically address:

Risks of Download

The enterprise-level system administrator shall have the responsibility and authority to limit downloading of software packages from the Internet, if that is in the best interest of the company.

Additionally, to protect against downloading viruses, organizational-level system administrators will instruct all employees to perform virus check on all files downloaded. This policy also addresses files that are attachments to E-Mail messages.

RB Enterprises employees shall:

1) Download files to a floppy disk and check for viruses before putting them on the computer's hard drive.

2) Perform a second check of the decompressed files if the originals are compressed files.

Problems of Virus Scanning

The system administrator will perform integrity checks, virus detection and removal, and immediately alert the company employees if any newer virus strains successfully penetrate virus scanning at the firewall or the desk top.

To establish further preventive security measures, the system administrator shall have the authority and responsibility to perform periodic checks for unacceptable use on those systems that allow remote access.

Support Resources

As noted earlier, the proliferation of electronic bulletin boards combined with the growth of the Internet, allows RB Enterprises to place information on Web servers which can be easily and legally accessed by the consumers. To reiterate the steps outlined under the Effective and Efficient Usage policy, RB Enterprises shall take great care to ensure that only properly reviewed and cleared information is placed on the Internet, inclusive of replies via electronic mail.

Who Authorizes Usage

In accordance with the policy stated under the subsection Web Pages Must Professionally Represent Enterprise, all RB Enterprises's Web servers connected to the Internet must receive authorization and approval by the enterprise WebMaster and the respective organizational-level WebMasters prior to being put into production. Failure to receive authorization will result in automatic disconnection from the Internet.

Who Maintains Web Presence

Refer to responsibilities addressed under subsection Web Pages Must Professionally Represent Enterprise.

Disciplinary Actions for Policy Violations

Supervisory and management personnel, and others with responsibility for Internet resources shall ensure that RB Enterprises's employees are informed of their responsibilities on the use of Internet. Employees are to avoid any use of the Internet services that violate the RB Enterprises's standards of conduct. Further, this directive states without any reservation that management will not tolerate prohibited uses of the Internet services on RB Enterprises resources, and violators will be subject to disciplinary action.

For disciplinary action, RB Enterprises will follow the approach endorsed by law enforcement and prosecutors. Under this approach, intruders will continue their activities at the site until the company apprehends the right person(s).

There is not global policy regarding the actual disciplinary action(s) to be taken. Such actions will be based on the severity of the damage, disruptions caused by the present and possibly future penetrations, attack frequency, financial or other risks to assets, and so forth.

HR managers shall ensure that all RB Enterprises's employees, especially those who are Internet users, know about the requirements set forth here.

Further, through periodic log-on messages, Enterprise WebMaster shall remind the Internet users of this requirement and their individual responsibilities under the law.

Policy Review Committee Representatives

Enterprise WebMaster, as stated under the subsection, Web Pages Must Professionally Represent Enterprise, shall form a policy review committee with appropriate representation from the various RB Enterprises's organizations. These representatives will have the authority to speak for their respective business areas. The committee will serve to review, interpret, and revise this policy directive, as required.

Appendix: Netiquette Tutorial

These are available from many vendors. Include the one that you feel is most comprehensive.

Corporate E-Mail and Security Policies

Include these as attachments to this directive. If you don't have anything written on these issues, you need to develop additional guidelines. [1]

There are two main sources from which the problems arise: from hardware and software malfunctions and from misuse by human beings. With the widespread use of the Internet which has the capability to link everything to unknown strangers, many enterprises have become newly vulnerable to human misuse of Internet services in the form of hacking, the creation of viruses, invasions of privacy, and so on. The above statement of policy concerning the proper use of the resources of the Internet only partially covers all of the major problem areas. Each enterprise planning to issue an Internet policy must work out more details on the technical and organizational interface responsibilities: What does the HR do? How does it coordinate with the legal affairs and security?

[1] The author thanks Oliver Smoot of ITA, Walter Okon of DISA, Mark Gordon, Christopher Gallinari, Barry Weiss, and Diana McKenzie of Gordon and Glickson Law Offices for their encouragement and support in the creation of this example on Internet Policy Directive. While he is grateful for the exchange of ideas with and contributions of those mentioned above, final responsibility for the style, content, and views expressed herein rests with the author.

Chapter 6

Additional Implementation Topics

"The boundaries that once separated information industries like computing, communications, and consumer electronics are disappearing. The result will be revolutionary changes in the way we deliver, receive, store, manipulate, share, and respond to information."

Sam Fuller, vice president
Corporate Research
Digital Equipment Corporation

THE THREE THEMES OF THE INTERNET

The preceding chapters underscored three key themes. First, it is important for enterprise decision makers to understand what is possible before instituting strategies and goals. To that end, chapter 3 provided some hypothetical scenarios to discuss what the Internet offers to ensure that manufacturing, healthcare, transportation, environmental monitoring, and other enterprises attain their respective visions.

The second theme is that strategies and goals, not the Internet technology, should receive priority considerations. Again, with hypothetical scenarios, chapter 4 provided insight on organizational networking and integration strategies and goals for improving cross-functional processes and applications. These strategies and goals should be aligned with and support an enterprise's strategic vision and opportunity. Access is empowerment; hence, the need for Internet technology!

The third theme is classification of payoff: economic, cost cutting, and strategic. It is difficult to measure real benefits, and it makes a difference whether one is examining global issues or individual applications. Chapter 5 implied that many Internet-related innovations may involve measuring something for the first time or in a way that differs from the past. There is a need to combine traditional and nontraditional systems of measurement, because a purely economic approach will not support vital but risky investments in an infrastructure that embraces an indefinable future model of operation.

CASE STUDIES

This chapter uses actual case studies as models to demonstrate how mission and business decisions drive the implementation and use of the Internet.

Commercial Enterprise and the Internet[1]

The first case deals with goal setting and the appraisal of the particular goal. The case mate-

---

[1] The author gratefully acknowledges the fine work of Sirkka Jarvenpaa of the University of Texas at Austin and Marvin Bower Fellow at Harvard Business School, and Blake Ives of Edwin L. Cox School, Southern Methodist University. The material for this section has been drawn from their initial effort in presenting Digital Equipment Corporation on the Internet. However, the author assumes full responsibility for any flaws that might have arisen in the presentation here.

rial pertains to the business concerns of a commercial enterprise as it evaluates the adoption of the Internet to leverage the technology *internally* to become more effective at shaping the enterprise's future. More specifically, it provides insight on how Digital Equipment Corporation (Digital) initially caught the wave of demand for Internet services within its own organization and enterprise, and then reset its business vision to dominate the market for firewalls and Internet security.

Kenneth Olsen founded Digital in 1957. Its inaugural product was the world's first inexpensive minicomputer, the PDP. By 1994, its product line encompassed several industry-focused solutions involving client/server computing, networking technology, and systems integration. It also contained support systems and services for Internet users. This latter category included relay points for newsgroup communication, public domain software for accessing remote files, and the CommerceNet information network that addresses the reliability, security, and access requirements for commercial exploitation of the Internet.

In 1994, Digital launched a comprehensive Internet Security Service which included a security consulting service and a new gateway software package. The gateway software package, called the Screening External Access Link (SEAL) firewall, was an internally developed, innovative solution to Digital's own security problems which posed a major barrier to its commerce on the Internet. It turned out to be a timely innovation, because it also met an immediate market demand for a security product wherever an enterprise sought to extend the functionality of its internal network with an Internet connectivity. CIOs worry about connecting their internal networks to the Internet. They need a secure gateway to link them to the rest of the world. Thus, the gateway became a product that would create a lucrative Internet business opportunity for Digital. The explosive growth of Mosaic and the World Wide Web helped Digital further define its vision, its strategies, and its goals for the Internet business.

Digital began to use Mosaic early in the spring of 1993 as a way to help the summer college interns look up information on the current work in the lab, the programming environment, and local interests during their stay. Digital previously compiled this type of information manually and then distributed the packages to the interns. In 1993, Digital decided to abandon this manual document preparation effort. Instead, it encouraged the interns to use Mosaic *inside* Digital as the basic source of information. This new method of information sharing and dissemination was welcomed at all the Digital research labs. Soon, they started several independent Web efforts. These internal Web server projects produced significant practical awareness about the benefits of hypertext links that permit the closer reviews of related projects, sharing of research results, accessing technical reports, and so on. But it was not until after Digital built, installed, and tested the World Wide Web relay within Digital's Internet firewall and permitted access to the external Web (i.e., the World Wide Web), that its employees were able to see the enormous business possibilities.

Russ Jones of Digital Corporate Communications used to provide Digital's information to the Internet newsgroups and bulletin boards which serve special interest groups. But once he saw the workings of Mosaic, he realized that this technology could be leveraged to project Digital all over the world—directly to the screens of Digital's customers. He then established Digital's external Web server to allow customers around the world access to 3,000 documents that included technical manuals and research reports. From there on, if anybody wanted to get up-to-date information on Digital, the Web was the place to go.

The information ranged from descriptions of hardware, software, and services to Digital's announcements about software patches and test running their applications in the new *Alpha AXP* computer that was sold as an Internet server. The customers could also configure systems, get price quotations, and, above all, place orders. Digital became the first computer industry vendor to offer *online ordering* of its full product line over the Internet. Initially, these services were limited to academic institutions and research laboratories, but in 1994, the same services were extended to a wider U.S. customer base, with plans for worldwide release.

Digital's management became more and more aware of the profit potential as they reviewed the reports that:

- by early 1994, more than 2,500 potential customers from twenty-seven countries had logged onto the external Web for a test drive;

- the city of Palo Alto Home Page attracted worldwide attention, so much so that a Silicon Valley competitor wanted to supplant Digital as the provider of the city's Web pages;

- Digital's product information and benchmarking services available on the Net produced $100 million in 1994 sales.

These reports supported a case for *engaging in Internet business*, rather than merely using it to achieve enterprise integration, marketing, advertising, and customer service objectives. However, by the end of fiscal year 1994 (June), Digital was reporting an annual net loss of over $2 billion. Bob Palmer, the president and CEO, was exploring avenues to bring the company back to profitability by the end of 1994. He publicly announced plans for selling noncore businesses. Given Digital's precarious financial condition, the company executives were not expected to be receptive to investment unless someone put forth a strong argument that the growing Internet-related business opportunity was a solution that they should act on quickly.

Sam Fuller, vice president of corporate research, had some early successes in that regard. He brought the Internet to senior executives' awareness in early 1993. A video presentation broadly promoted the Internet benefits both inside and outside of Digital. It was a brief three-minute presentation, but it previewed Digital's position at the forefront of Web-based business transformation. It demonstrated how global electronic commerce was taking place on the Net and how the key players were congregating. More importantly, it clearly articulated two points. First, the communication vendors undermine the validity of the Internet by referring to future possibilities. Secondly, global electronic commerce was already in evidence and Digital was occupying a leading part in this new way of doing business.

By March 1994, executive support for the Internet improved to the extent that Bob Palmer made a keynote presentation at the UNIX trade show, UniForm. He took advantage of the video and gave an online demonstration of Mosaic and the World Wide Web. Several thousand people, including a number of CEOs, saw the presentation. They were impressed, and a flurry of sales leads were generated.

Now that the Internet business looked promising, the challenge for Digital was to define its own unique products and services for this emerging business environment. As of 1994, Digital's strengths were in client/server computing, networking technology, and systems integration. Its products were scalable Alpha AXP systems, storage, networking, software, and services, as well as industry-focused solutions that were increasingly offered in partnership with third party vendors. The Internet did not exactly fit in with any of Digital's existing business units, but it did have implications for most. So, the following questions had to be addressed:

1) Should the Internet business be structured as an independent, functional business?

2) Should it run horizontally across the existing businesses, creating, demands for other Digital products such as consulting services, servers workstations, etc.? Would such an arrangement avoid interdivisional competition?

3) In terms of the business model, Would people ask for Digital's services basically to access the Internet, to protect themselves, to redesign networks, and to set up the Web servers?

4) Would the real opportunity arise from business reengineering, education, and integration with legacy systems?

Based on Digital's strategic market assessment, the executive management ascertained that the real Internet opportunities would be with those who want to buy and sell information, products, and services at the desk tops and in their homes. The value-added service that could be provided here would be *to make all this easy to do*. The market is huge and so are the challenges in it, which are characterized by diversity, heterogeneity, and multiple operating systems and platforms. Further, the Digital executives analyzed the three legs to the Internet-related business, identifying the key players in each in an attempt to evaluate and justify Digital's profit potential in any one or more of these business environment(s):

REVIEW

Connectivity—AT&T or MCI in partnership with others have a real opportunity to dominate in this domain.

Content Providers—Everybody wants to be a publisher. The success potential is as great for Dun and Bradstreet or the *Wall Street Journal* as it is for anybody else.

Commerce Enablers—These provide expertise in transaction management and processing. This is where Digital has an upper edge. SEAL provides security to businesses, and a modified version allows for home use, thereby enabling Digital to offer what people need to get on the Internet.

According to the executives at its Cambridge Research Lab, Digital was three to nine months ahead of other large computer companies in the Internet marketplace. However, staying ahead of the pack means the company must be ready to innovate at an unprecedented pace. Such innovation will impact both the product design and marketing/distribution strategies. Ellen Kokos of Digital explains that the Web technology becomes increasingly exciting when interactive media capability is added. However, strictly from a business standpoint, the profitability of product design can only be measured in terms of its ability to reach the widest possible audience. She hastens to point out that not everyone has a 486 on her or his desk at home or in the office. This implies that if Digital wants to capitalize on its existing edge and remain competitive in the Internet business environment, it must do so with the knowledge that Internet product design will continue to be a challenge. Similarly, in the marketing/distribution environment, it must recognize other innovative approaches that are at play. A pull model suggests a series of hierarchical pack-ages—you can order a basic product for, let us say, a mere $100; to provide a necessary add-on feature, the supplier can incrementally increase the price by $300; and then there could be various consulting services for an additional $1,000+ a month. The *Economist* magazine suggests: "One has to advertise by pushing free teasers out and let customers pull for the revenue-generating items."

Digital recognized the currency of this marketing/distribution practice. It decided to com-pete in the Internet market by:

- providing access to the Internet;

- providing protection;

- redesigning the network and setting up Web server services, which would include business reengineering, education, and integration with legacy systems.

Digital entered the Internet market with the basic understanding that businesses wanted to implement the above type of programs in bite-size chunks. With Internet technology, cus-tomers have the option of starting small and building up slowly. So, the $250,000 deals could appear in the sequence of $25,000. Given this awareness about the Internet tech-nology and the fact that it is here today—it is fundamental as fax machines, phones, air-lines, and trains—and it is not going to go away, Digital devised new business strategies and goals to add value and make money from a resource perceived by many as free, and profit from high volume commodity products. Its Internet suc-cesses to-date include:

REVIEW

Enterprise Integration

- internet security product;

- heavy internal use of the World Wide Web and the Internet as an information resource as well as a communication capa-bility;

- use of the World Wide Web to disseminate marketing infor-mation to customers throughout the world;

- use of the Internet as a direct sales channel through the electronic connection as well as for distributing software patches;

- a first-in-the-industry program, allowing Internet users worldwide to test drive free Alpha AXP server computers, and

Internet-related Business

- a strategic partner in Internet-based innovations such as MecklerWeb and CommerceNet;

- bundling of Mosaic Internet navigation software with all Digital computer systems;

- development of a number of Web-based applications with large customers.

Medical Education/Public Information and the Internet

Chapter 3 previewed the health-care industry and how it could benefit from the power and resources of the Internet. These resources could be useful not only for medical professionals, but also for the general public, as long as the information and resources are considered to be a library of information and not a substitute for a visit to the physician. The second case study pertains to the instructional resources being put on the Internet by those who share a common concern for physician education, public health, and the environment.[2]

As the interest for pursuing health-care-related information exchanges over the Internet grows, the issue of providing data security to protect confidential health records is frequently brought up for discussion. Had we reviewed and analyzed the topic of medical information exchanges on real patients and their health records by the hospitals, physicians, regulatory, and insurance professionals, such discussion would warrant immediate

---

[2] This section is drawn from the various case studies that the U.S. Department of Health and Human Services, Public Health Service Division puts on the Internet. The author gratefully acknowledges the other published reference information that Dr. Keith Phillips, William Bebout, Leslie Campbell, and Jim Martindale provided. The information covered here basically illustrates the point that medicine can benefit greatly from the power and resources of the Internet. The material is assumed to be accurate, but any information taken from this case study must be verified by a qualified medical professional for its relevance and currency.

attention to the appropriate use of key technologies for data security. To allay the fears of security conscious individuals, it is important to state that medical researchers can use, as and when needed, the mechanism for authentication, which ensures that information sent on a network has not been altered, and encryption, which makes data unreadable without the use of a password or electronic key. This discussion, however, centers around *information exchanges for medical education and public awareness*. Such information is considered public domain information and does not require the highest level of security precautions.

The American Academy of Family Physicians, American Academy of Pediatrics, American College of Emergency Physicians, American College of Occupational and Environmental Medicine, American Medical Association, Association of State and Territorial Health Officials, and the Society of Teachers of Family Medicine in association with the Agency for Toxic Substances and Disease Registry (ATSDR) provide instructions on the Internet to increase the primary care provider's knowledge of hazardous substances in the environment and to aid in the evaluation of potentially exposed patients. Their materials address arsenic, asbestos, benzene, radon, lead, and such other poisoning substances.

This case study deals with ATSDR and how it disseminates the information on lead poisoning throughout the United States on the Net, what it covers, and why such publication is timely, productive, and worthwhile. ATSDR materials provide immediate sources of information on how a wide variety of workers, hobbyists, and substance abusers may encounter potentially high levels of lead. These include detailed information about the occupational, environmental, substance use, hobby, and other sources of lead exposure, including certain folk remedies. Further, challenging questions instruct what to ask the patient and his or her family in order to evaluate less obvious, but possible, sources of lead exposure. Evaluations and treatment protocols cover important topics such as what would likely be revealed by an X-ray of the abdomen or long bones of a lead-exposed child; how lead is distributed among blood, soft tissue (kidney, bone marrow, liver, and brain), and mineralizing tissue (bone and teeth); how the body accumulates this metal over a lifetime and releases it slowly; what is related to the risk of adverse effects, and so on.

Physiological and neurological effects are also clearly enumerated. For instance, the most sensitive target of lead poisoning is the nervous system. In children, neurological deficits could occur at exposure levels once thought to cause no harmful effects. Besides, childhood toxicity could have permanent effects. ATSDR materials provide linkage to a number of Evidence Based Medicine Working Groups and other information services on the Internet that track continued deficits in neurological development, psychometric intelligence scores, speech and language processing, attention, and classroom performance of children exposed to different levels of lead poisoning.

There are additional reviews of hematologic, endocrine, renal, reproductive, and developmental effects, as well as carcinogenic effects. These provide up to date information on the major effects of lead on the human body and how lead's effects differ in children and adults. For treatments, the materials give instructions on clinical evaluation beginning with basic history and physical examination to signs and symptoms, with specifics on mild, moderate, and severe cases of lead toxicity. Guidance is provided on laboratory tests to evaluate CBC with peripheral smear, blood lead level, erythrocyte protoporphyrin level, BUN and creatinine level, and urinanalysis. Under each of these tests, there are valuable medical insights. For instance, under CBC with peripheral smear, important medical observations are included: in a lead-poisoned patient, the hematocrit and hemoglobin values may be slightly to moderately low. The differential and total white count may appear normal. The peripheral smear may be either normochromic and normocytic or hypochromic and microcytic. Other evidence crucial for patients who have been significantly poisoned for a prolonged period is clearly identified with detailed discussion of blood lead test results and follow-up activities.

Regarding treatment and management, ATSDR materials discuss the steps after diagnosing lead poisoning. These include the identification and correction of dietary deficiencies, and education of family members on the preventable hazards of lead and on appropriate therapy. ATSDR materials are comprehensive in that they give appropriate considerations to several drug tests used in the treatment of lead poisoning by articulating clearly the potential side effects of these drugs and what, if any, caution must be exercised in prescribing and using these drugs. There are references to federal standards and regulations that differentiate what lead levels are mandated and what are only recommended. For instance, the federal lead standard specifies the permissible exposure limit of lead in the workplace, the frequency and extent of medical monitoring, and other responsibilities of the employer. ATSDR materials review the Occupational Safety and Health Administration (OSHA) standards for the amount of lead allowed in workroom air over an eight-hour workday, Environmental Protection Agency's (EPA) ambient air standard for lead and goal for lead in drinking water after treatment, and so forth. Further, ATSDR reports on Food and Drug Administration (FDA) goals, and Consumer Product Safety Commission limits in paints intended for residential use or for bridges and marine use.

Several states require primary care physicians to report cases of lead poisoning. ATSDR materials identify the appropriate health agencies so that abatement of lead sources, education of the patient, and remediation measures can be instituted. Further, the materials discuss what the laboratories performing blood lead tests in several states are required to do, if they detect abnormal results.

To make the materials entirely instructional, appropriate answers to all the questions are included, and there are post-test questions, too. In this piece, we covered only one case of environmental hazard: lead toxicity. ATSDR maintains an online catalog of several other hazardous substance-related information. For public health reasons, this timely availability of information is crucial, because knowledge regarding the treatment of patients potentially exposed to these substances in the environment is constantly evolving and is often uncertain. ATSDR published information is an additional resource for physicians and other health professionals in assessing the condition and managing the treatment.

ATSDR is one of the many medical resources on the Internet. Other resources are available to facilitate medical research and education. For instance, Martindale's Health Science Guide—'95 is a "Medical Multimedia Education and Specialized Information Resource Center." It is considered to be among the top 5percent of all Web sites. It provides connectivity to metabolic pathways and genetic maps, interactive anatomy browsers, online medical journals, text books and tutorials, cases and teaching files, and so forth. These, together with several others, feed the planning process with six categories of benefits:

1) Availability of information

2) Higher efficiency in healthcare information management and dissemination

   a) Documentation

   b) Space management

   c) Elimination of duplication

3) Clinical Benefits—Information Sharing

4) Epidemiological benefits

5) Cost savings

   a) Administrative and management

   b) Documentation

   c) Space costs

   d) Medical care savings

6) Better quality care

These benefits aid the healthcare provider with "what if" scenarios, statistics, and trend analysis, and must be interpreted together with other sources of authority. These are *not* substitutes for professional services rendered by the physicians and other healthcare providers.

This case study is not complete without an analysis of the most important payoff from investment in Internet publication. The reader is reminded of the problem of measuring the incommensurable. Earlier in chapter 5, there were a few illustrations on how to identify and measure benefits that are not strictly quantifiable. There was a special reference to information as management. A technique was suggested to measure Management Productivity in order to determine if an enterprise is handling information to address customer service problems. That approach needs to be invoked here to reiterate a crucial point: For ATSDR or organizations such as the National Institute of Health (NIH), or National Science Foundation (NSF), payoff will not appear in the balance sheet, but among more qualitative measures of public health concerns. How does the Internet technology further the ATSDR or NIH's mission? How does it help the institution meet the needs of its community for relevant environmental courses and public awareness services? How does it increase both the community's need for access and ATSDR, NIH, or NSF's ability to share up-to-date information and resources with others?

To the extent that the Internet becomes second nature to the primary care physician's operational and educational purposes and more precisely fits these functions, it can assure institutions such as ATSDR, NIH, or NSF of their relevancy in a rapidly changing world and allow them to contribute to medical health-care education's evolving, and increasingly important role in society. As primary care physicians and other health-care professionals learn to use the medical alerts and other resources on the Internet to respond to the particular needs of the community, ATSDR, NIH, NSF, and other agencies and institutions become more effective at protecting the community's health and enhancing the lives of those afflicted with health problem—surely the most satisfying payoff of all.

Chapter **7**

Summary and Analysis: Internet and the Enabling Technologies

HIGHLIGHTS

This book represents a milestone in the strategic assessment of the Internet and World Wide Web usage. Through numerous case histories, the preceding parts have validated that the Internet revolution is upon us. Countless organizations are exploring how they can best use the Internet, in particular the World Wide Web, for business applications such as marketing, supply chain management, public relations, consumer support, product sales, and electronic data interchange. Further, the book underscores the point that sound information is of critical importance to help businesses understand the Internet opportunities. To that end, the different chapters address the critical information need by examining what is occurring on the Internet, what Internet means, where it is going, and how to leverage this new opportunity. If these discussions change the various entities' perspectives on Internet opportunities and form the foundation for their planning cycle for Internet deployment, the author will have achieved his purpose and goals.

The book incorporates numerous survey results of the Internet users and their perception of the benefits of interactive activities on the World Wide Web. A large number of questions must be answered before the Internet is widely accepted by CEOs, CFOs, and other key decision makers and organizations as a key means for conducting business. Numerous surveys are routinely conducted to accurately profile Internet users. These surveys, while timely and useful, have two drawbacks. First, they focus on Internet users, while they exclude people who are not connected, such as many CEOs and CFOs. Secondly, these surveys tend to be proprietary, which limits the availability of the study results to those few who might know about them through their sponsorship or some other means. However, these survey results uncover numerous ideas relevant to the promotion and acceleration of the use of the Internet. For instance, a majority of the people still think of the Internet as simply E-Mail, but Table 7.1 depicts how some people find plenty of other business uses for the Internet.

This is the first Internet book that has sought to redefine and clarify individuals', businesses', and organizations' understanding of the use and possibilities of the Internet. It has done so by reviewing survey results from various sources, taking them apart and then putting them back together again with other decision tools, and making the final product readily available to the industry as a whole. The result is benchmark strategic assessment. This provides, in certain special areas, projectable information such as Return On Management (R-O-M) Productivity. This new measuring index serves as a means to plan Internet deployment; further, it serves as a baseline against which to compare future profitability of the public or private business concerns.

USED	PERCENT OF WWW USERS WHO HAVE USED IT FOR BUSINESS PURPOSES
COLLABORATING WITH OTHERS	54%
PUBLISHING INFORMATION	33%
GATHERING INFORMATION	77%
RESEARCHING COMPETITORS	46%
SELLING PRODUCTS OR SERVICES	13%
PURCHASING PRODUCTS OR SERVICES	23%
PROVIDING CUSTOMER SERVICE AND SUPPORT	38%
COMMUNICATING INTERNALLY	44%
PROVIDING VENDOR SUPPORT AND COMMUNICATIONS	50%

Source: "The CommerceNet/Nielsen Internet Demographics Survey," Nielsen Interactive Services—Press Release, February 1996, http://www.nielsenmedia.com/whatsnew/execsum2.html

Table 7.1: Business Uses of the WWW

In the marketplace today, most enterprises are taking a great deal of pleasure in providing free information to others. This trend is likely to continue in the Internet but within that framework, it is also possible for for-profit exchanges of information to coexist with the free ones. Such a balance is what enterprises must develop to derive the maximum benefit out of "the bits that slip across the borders through the Internet medium without much fanfare."[1] This section summarizes the key issues and challenges that the author chose to tackle to define the operational and administrative coordination that enterprises must achieve to find the balance.

DETAILS

The book tackles several issues and challenges simultaneously. It is a topic and issue oriented book, designed for CEOs, CFOs, CIOs, and managers. It supplements the more tool/task-oriented user guides which cover the gamut of Internet tools and services and include resource directories.

Chapter 1 of the book defines the:

1) Background and origin of the Internet

2) Present and future of the two important facets which comprise the Internet technology environment:

   • Use of Internet technologies external to an enterprise

   • Use of Internet technologies within an enterprise, i.e., Intranet

3) More technical aspects of using

   • Electronic Mail

   • Network Newsgroups
   —FTP
   —Telnet
   —The World Wide Web

   • The leading Internet search-and-query tools
   —Gopher
   —Wide Area Information Service (WAIS)
   —Veronica
   —Archie, etc.

4) Information Distribution, i.e., connectivity providers

5) Information access, i.e., security issues.

Internet is no longer merely providing transport and access; rather, as chapter 2 discusses, the Internet is shaping the way businesses and consumers worldwide communicate, learn, entertain, shop, and even heal. chapter 2 makes it clear that we are entering the age of ambitious applications, combining audio, video, and data traffic in the Internet setting [2]. It states systematically and comprehensively that Internet tackles problems of corporate communications, physical plants, and even geography. Through appropriate examples, chapter 2 illustrates that there is hardly an industry or government service (e.g., manufacturing, healthcare, transportation, and environmental monitoring) that cannot address its great challenges through the Internet. There are factual details on just how pervasive the Internet has become as a critical business tool, as well as indications of how wide and creative Internet applications are. For instance, in the section about manufacturing, there are references to auto manufacturers that leverage the Internet to create virtual offices and factories supported by twenty-four-hour-a-day research or development facilities. They are engineering automobiles around the clock by sending information back and forth through the Net among work sites in Detroit, Europe, and Asia. The discussion further creates the awareness that virtual factories allow a company to build any product at any time just about anywhere in the world. Several instances highlight how the dramatic reduction in cycle time from order to delivery is reduced. Statistics could easily be produced to show that today more than 40 percent of all U.S. manufacturers are electronically linked to their suppliers, partners, and customers, thereby creating greater efficiency and, more importantly, closer bonds.

In illustrating the health-care industry, material was presented to infer that the Internet revolution has made the virtual hospital and doctor's office an immediate reality. Today, health-care professionals can easily overcome the constraints of time and distance to conduct medical evaluations. Chapter 2 makes clear that interactive multimedia networks will soon link hospital administrators, physicians, and health-care providers around the world to perform even surgical procedures whenever and wherever needed. Equally productive, timely, and profitable are the activities of the transportation business. In this sector, an entity is able to create the foundation for a very aggressive and profitable venture by combining the big company's asset—a powerful direct sales force—with the Internet and other software capabilities. A case in point is the airline industry. It is committed to bringing the best in online access and content to its crew and customers [3]. Likewise, environmental monitoring activities are poised to provide their client base with volumes of previously inaccessible environmental data and model information through the Internet to form virtual teams or outright partnerships to address environmental issues on a global scale.

To summarize chapter 2, the above sectors and their particular examples are just a sprinkling of what the Internet can do for businesses and consumers. What is crucial is to understand that content takes many shapes. The content will change dramatically as broadband delivery improves the nature of the Internet medium. If you, as a CEO or CFO, decide to go online, you should start thinking about exploiting the uniqueness of this medium by directing your customers to go to places within the Internet that your enterprise can define and develop for targeted information and communications. That's what Internet is all about—the winners will be the enterprises that exploit the Web environment in particular. The challenge is to make it a more robust, comprehensive, and usable medium which business users would like to access in order to look for fresh ideas and new products and services. Most of the Web sites are used to make company information available to users.

Chapter 3 discusses how enterprises can use the Internet formats to simplify their general communications need. There are two issues here—internal and external communications. Because *internal* Web sites are just emerging, chapter 3 does not immediately identify and differentiate the two separate application potentials. Rather, it discusses how currently used communication vehicles that are too limited to cope with today's market environment could be subsumed by the Web technology for both the enterprise applications and external applications. It suggests that intuitive access to broad types of media makes the Web an ideal solution to the communication problems. As more companies are realizing its superiority, the number of internal Web sites is quietly growing [4]. Through appropriate scenarios, chapter 3 suggests that the range of applications that can be developed to meet industry-specific or general needs is virtually limitless. As illustrated by the airline company example, Internet applications can facilitate:

- One-to-many communications: teams, departments, or entire corporations can set up pages where they post information, thereby reducing bulky, easily outdated paper-based information. Applications like this bring an immediate payback to organizations by reducing costs of updating corporate information.

- Two-way interactions such as crew members checking schedule options, vacation balances, and benefits information. When an employee needs a report or a personalized letter, using Web technology linked to legacy data can be an intuitive and efficient alternative to the delays and frustrations of multiple, incompatible E-Mail systems within the same company environment.

- Many-to-many interactions for direct exchanges of information between members of a group, making information available to others within the group.

These types of Web applications improve communications and productivity across all areas of a company. They vary in forms depending on whether they are designed to meet the needs of specific departments or corporatewide functions. For instance, in discussing an airline company's sales and marketing activities, chapter 3 notes that there is a great demand to liaise with an often geographically distributed group of people to obtain up-to-date and reference information on:

- Pricing
- Product information, including special seasonal offers so that sales is aware of planned marketing activities and sales forecasts
- Key competitive information

The first important message of chapter 3 is that Web-based internal applications can give immediate access to these types of reference information. As the Internet continues to mature into the mainstream platform for computing, internal Web sites will require better application development tools. In that regard, industry trends provide reason for great optimism. Some of the tools by leading vendors are being used to improve the way companies link people and the corporate information sources within private companywide Webs. Accordingly, leading companies are readily adopting the internal Web site development idea to deliver an unprecedented and powerful combination of openness and security, intuitive access to highly graphical information, and flexibility for customization.

For external communications, the World Wide Web and individual Web sites offer individuals and corporations access to large amounts of invaluable information. Many corporations have been quick to realize that this easy access to rich information can benefit customer service and support groups by enabling them to:

- Share up-to-date status reports on problems so that all team members can respond to customer calls

- Act immediately on any important changes, such as special opportunities or problems

- Respond in real-time to customer queries and complaints

Chapter 3 documents numerous applications of external Web sites such as purchasing, advertising, product development, human resources, finance, and so forth. While the scenario discusses applications related to airlines and transport, there are also other industries including aerospace, investment banking, telecommunication, entertainment, manufacturing, and computer software and hardware companies, which are convinced of the advantages of external Web applications. These companies have implemented WWW applications and report significant improvements in staff productivity [5].

Therefore, the second important message of chapter 3 is that WWW offers powerful capabilities to conduct simultaneous internal communications by allowing migration of Internet to corporate networks, i.e., Intranet, as well as encrypted communications and electronic commerce on the Internet. "Encrypted communications" bring to the surface several issues and challenges that must be dealt with to ensure the continued growth of this remarkable medium. One of the most pressing issues confronting the growth of the Internet for external communications and transactions is simply fear. Chapter 3 omits any discussion on this aspect, because many critics raise the issue in many different ways and the opinions are based on assumptions, rather than objective analysis of the actual Internet environment. To summarize the issues and concerns and address specific solutions, a thorough review of evolving features and standards is required to determine what are likely to simplify communications and give confidence in conducting business on the Internet. Such a review is beyond the scope of this book. Nonetheless, it is important to offer some guidelines in these matters.

Some talk about losing privacy or personal contact with others, becoming overwhelmed by information, facing new learning curves, or other fears. The author concurs with many of the industry leaders that Internet access and content providers are mindful that people and businesses are looking for a simple, reliable, productive, entertaining, consistent, comfortable, and easy Internet environment in which to work and play [6]. Since Internet is a many-to-many communications medium, users perceive that they are discovering each other rather than becoming concerned, frustrated, and alienated. On the planning and operational aspect, the users are beginning to see:

- basic organization of information on the Internet;
- search mechanisms to index the content of Web sites;
- a search capability at the elemental level with information drawn from a combination of E-Mail, newsgroups, wire services, and home pages [7].

These are not things to come in the distant future; rather, these facilities are available today. More refinement is needed, and the industry leaders rightly state that the seeds of solution lie inside the network or lie inside the technology [8]. This statement applies equally to the other frequently mentioned fear that Internet is insecure. No one is better prepared than Jim Clark, president of Netscape Communications, to address this problem.[1] Netscape Navigator represents more than 85 percent of usage on the World Wide Web, according to a variety of Internet sites such as The Internet Financial Database, The Scripps Research Institute, TISC, and the University of Illinois at Urbana-Champaign. Netscape includes encryption technologies which, together with secure-web capability, firewalls, and filtering routers from other vendors, safeguard financial transactions and electronic commerce [9]. Clark affirms that security protection is being solved in many respects by the Internet rather than being violated by the Internet. Clark and other industry leaders think we are witnessing a new transformation in security technology solutions. Each and every time someone has a network connection, a piece of software can check to

---

[1] In 1995, two computer science students at the University of California at Berkeley cracked the Public-key encryption code used by Netscape Communications Corporation's popular browser software to protect information transmitted over the Net. However, the problem was easily fixed.

see if the connection has permission to run—that is, whether or not connection has been paid for. This verification, plus cryptography certificates, digital signatures, and other mechanisms that are emerging on the Net, can wrap any piece of content in a computer program which requires permission to be used. This assurance is imperative as more and more organizations go online to conduct business.[2]

A very rich market is evolving out of the Internet, and some of the services will be paid by subscription, pay-per-view, or pay-per-use. Everything imaginable that has to do with communication will occur over this network. Industry leaders are working closely with world-class partners to design and build industry-specific and customized superior security technology solutions that are at once compelling and solid for everything from banks, insurance companies, and securities firms, to global trade, financial, manufacturing, and other services organizations [11].

From the point of view of CEOs, CFOs, CIOs, and other decision makers, understanding the Internet phenomenon means we must look at both perceived added-value and real-added value. Through case studies, chapter 4 defines the scope of value-added service as the incredible customer value and control that could be had by a particular application tool. Business-to-business communications through E-Mail or file transfers are very important applications on the Internet. There is a range of other tools which improve communications, allow new customers to be reached, and enhance the enterprise's image. As discussed in chapter 3, these tools run very well in an Internet environment. Many enterprise decision makers are confident that the Internet environment, as a distributed entity of people who cooperate to produce better customer value and profitability, enhances management productivity. Businesses spend billions of dollars on maintaining their worldwide proprietary internal networks based on lease lines and other things. The important point is that the Internet has evolved into an enterprise infrastructure capable of solving these problems and improving management productivity.

Chapter 4 includes insightful analysis on the implications of using particular techniques for evaluating returns on enterprise infrastructure investment. Empirical investigations show that return on equity, return on assets, and other traditional financial metrics have failed to yield a positive correlation between business performance and information technology infrastructure investment. This has caused the productivity paradox: it has been difficult to understand why some companies succeed with information technology investments yielding revenue growth, while others fail. Paul Strassmann argues that it is not the willy-nilly application of information technology, but its proper management that

2 *InformationWeek* and Ernst &Young surveyed 1,293 IS executives in October 1995. According to this survey, 70 percent of companies already protect themselves on the Net with firewalls; about 60 percent with virus protection and passwords; and 15 percent with encryption [10].

encourages productivity. Internet allows the proper management of information. If management is the key to the productivity of organizations, Strassmann advocates that measuring management productivity would open the way to exploring the benefits of Internet being used by its principal customers, the managers of information. Chapter 4 recommends a technique for deriving a Return on Management (R-O-M) Productivity Index.

This technique is addressed to those CEOs, CFOs, CIOs and other executives who are trying to extract the business value from their investments in information technologies. After applying the technique, these executives should have greater confidence in deploying Internet in assisting their enterprise to achieve its goals. To illustrate how Strassmann calculates value-added, two of his pioneering works: *1993 Information Productivity(TM) Rankings, Industrial Companies; and Introduction to R-O-M Analysis; Linking Management Productivity and Information Technology*, are included in Appendix A.

Chapter 5 sets the guidelines and tactics that the management of an enterprise should apply to allow for productive use of the Internet facilities by all employees. These guidelines should be reviewed and adapted by the various enterprises based on their unique business practices, procedures, and environments. The intention of chapter 5 is to provide an ethical standard to measure management productivity of enterprises with respect to the Internet and the related multicast communications network.[3] As such, the standard represents rights and responsibilities that belong to every Internet user of an enterprise. For instance, an enterprise policy should not infringe upon the right to:

- access any publicly available information, as long as it does not cost the enterprise any money;

- accept any information from any source;

- transform in any way any information an enterprise employee originates or receives;

- transmit any information to any person, if there is not any violation of the intellectual property rights;

- publish information in public forums and submit information to moderated forums, unless there is a violation of the intellectual property rights;

---

[3] The author is grateful to Monique C. M. Leahy and Peter Merel for the added insight he obtained from the works of these two experts on mishandled computer/Internet information.

- distribute in electronic form any publicly available report, policy, regulation, or law;

- deny participation, as a forum moderator, to any enterprise employee, unless limited by contractual obligations;

- seek legal recourse for damages caused by the actions and expressions of others.

There are responsibilities that must be stated and understood to exercise the above individual rights. Chapter 5, therefore, attempts to codify the collective responsibility of an enterprise. It proposes a template of model policies for handling situations whereby an organization could suffer loss of reputation and revenue due to its employees' breach of conduct in the Internet environment. The policies are directed at the employees to increase their awareness that it is their responsibility to:

- represent themselves, their observations and opinions, and the expressions of others sincerely and without misrepresentation;

- neither harass nor threaten others;

- include adequate warning with anyinformation that may mislead or endanger a naive reader;

- observe and enforce the charters of forums that they may moderate;

- observe, discuss, refine, and promote the rights and responsibilities represented in an enterprise's Internet policy document;

- pursue all conversational remedies for perceived damages and inequities before seeking judicial recourse;

- be considerate of the costs of network bandwidth and storage space.

The Internet medium is still undergoing testing and evaluation. Accordingly, the enterprises must recognize that most people on the Internet do not intend to offend others. If a correction is given to employees of an organization in pleasant and polite terms, they are more likely to listen to reason. In cases of recalcitrance, these policies may be enforced more rigorously if the offense becomes serious or sufficiently reprehensible with attendant loss of corporate revenues.

On that last point, Peter Merel's remarks are useful for enterprise decision makers in appreciating the complexity of this administrative task [12]. He observes that the main obstacle in enforcing appropriate practice on the Internet is that there is no way to know for sure who originates material, nor is there a way to know for sure that material has been transformed.

The state of technology is such that individuals can authenticate the information they originate, but it cannot verify that an Internet account or address is actually being used by the person registered as the operator. The problem is that anyone can purchase an Internet account and represent himself or herself as someone else, if he or she chooses to do so. Besides, the technology does not compel users to authenticate themselves. If an enterprise is facing an Internet abuse situation by one or more employees, it might be difficult to identify them.

Perhaps the best approach to curbing Internet abuse lies in:

1) raising employee awareness of the benefits of Internet participation;

2) explaining the tremendous commercial and professional opportunities that the Internet offers, and

3) presenting an unbiased view of the enterprise Internet technology and culture to dissuade employees from sensationalistic distortions by the broadcast media promotions.

If these low-key Internet policy enforcement options that rely basically upon the common sense and goodwill of an enterprise's Internet community fail, the enterprise system administrator can use other forms of discouragement, which are Internet culture derived penalties, to correct offensive behavior within the enterprise [13]. These, in effect, prevent an offender from accessing the Internet.[4] They seem to work, and at this point, it is not evident that any other penalties are required to add force to them. With that underlying consideration for the initial public relations effort, the model policy statements of Chapter 5 can be adjusted to support the development of new services that enhance an enterprise's use of the Internet as a general-purpose means of access into many business applications.

Chapter 6 summarizes lessons learned from the early adopters of the Internet. The first case history documents the evolutionary path of an in-house enterprise Web program at Digital Equipment Corporation. A grassroots project, championed by one or two employ-

---

[4] "Kill-file," "Mailbomb,"etc., are noncriminal sanctions that can be applied for noncompliance with a code of practice. These can effectively prevent offenders from accessing the Internet. Reference 13 provides the necessary details on how these Internet culture driven punitive actions work.

ees, soon attracted many users on the corporate network to warrant the attention of the CEO and Digital's strategic market assessment.

The planning or the strategic market assessment is really secondary to the process. In most situations, Webs grow in unexpected ways, often expanding beyond their initial focus. Digital's experience is no exception. There are several other corporations that started with the same modest goals. Some of them, such as the biotechnology giant Genentec, wanted to merely replace homegrown bulletin-board systems. They started with a shoestring budget only to report that the internal Web had grown rapidly and become very popular in a short span of time.

After reading such success stories, some of you might think of jump-starting the process in your own enterprises. By signing a major agreement with Netscape Communications Corporation, Lockheed Martin Enterprise Information Systems in Orlando, Florida is essentially validating the recent trend to plan to reach a large population rapidly at a fairly low cost [14]. Like Digital's initial Web site, Lockheed Martin plans to put its corporate phone directory, information on training programs, and many of its human resources documents on the site. These are relatively static documents and are not mission-critical to the company's business from an operational standpoint. Digital's case history illustrated that going beyond this static publishing model is a natural progression. Accordingly, it is no surprise that Lockheed Martin also plans to extend the use of the Web browsers to provide access to other business applications.

Such extensions typically bring about some changes; henceforth, individuals and departments will be responsible for publishing and maintaining the information that they will create with newer business applications. From an enterprise's standpoint, this transfer of responsibility creates two challenges. First, an enterprise will have to grant rights to the various departments and even individuals to create content. Secondly, it must put in place a policy and procedures document that entrusts someone (e.g., System Administrator or a WebMaster) to oversee that the content is "appropriate."

Lockheed Martin may have taken a progressive stance. It is allowing each department to design its own page, as long as it leverages information and reflects corporate culture. It has put in place policy and procedures guidelines that will run 200 to 300 pages [15].

Different enterprises will approach these challenges in different ways. In conclusion, the most compelling reasons for this book are:

1) to instruct the various enterprise decision makers to open up the
   Internet and get employees excited about using this technology envi-

ronment inside the enterprise (as described in chapter 3—"High Performance Business Team");

2) to teach employees that the internal Web is a superset of the external public one, and management should be looking after a common goal of corporate profitability (as discussed in chapter 4—"Taking New Measures"); and finally,

3) to advise that the enterprises should enforce appropriate behavior in the enterprise Internet system or environment. chapter 5 addresses the specific concerns with the aid of a model enterprise policy and procedures guide. It is a simple model, but has great potential to address all kinds of informational transactions over the Internet.

These fundamentally important dimensions will enrich enterprises enormously as they begin to use the Internet environment. The mutual efforts of employees within various enterprises will lead to the discovery of new territories for Internet applications and help create a future for these enterprises. It is incumbent upon these enterprises to create their own plans for exploiting the electronic space, along with appropriate "guidebooks" for enterprise Internet policy and procedures.

APPENDIX A

Definitions

Chapter 5 discussed why it is imperative to link the spending to business goals; it also elaborated on how twenty-first century consultants like Paul Strassmann, of New Canaan, Connecticut, are applying basic economic concepts of value to their understanding of what makes Information Technology (IT) pay. Strassmann defines the ratio of management value added to management costs as Return On Management (R-O-M). This ratio yields a positive correlation between business performance and IT investment. It captures the entire scope of the organizational changes being proposed.

Fortune 1000 companies such as Coca-Cola, AT&T, Quaker Oats, and others are using the R-O-M technique and in some instances, tying executive compensation to that data. The author wanted to supplement the basic definition of this ratio given in Chapter 5 with additional information, particularly in the realm of linking management productivity and information technology, where two of Strassmann's publications, "Introduction to R-O-M Analysis" and "1993 Information Productivity Rankings, Industrial Companies," were invaluable.

Strassmann has licensed his R-O-M technique to the consulting firm of Ernst & Young and his publications are widely distributed on the Internet. The above referenced articles are reproduced here with his permission.

Introduction to ROM® Analysis:
Linking Management Productivity and Information Technology

by Paul A. Strassmann

Contents

Strategic Business Report

Management Productivity Report

 Employment Characteristics
 The Management or Operations Categories
 Employment Table
 Cost Structure Tables

Click here to see the Information Productivity(tm) rankings of 549 companies from 1993.

Click to return to the Strassmann, Inc. home page.

Introduction

There is no relationship between expenses for computers and business profitability. Similar computer technologies can lead either to monumental successes or to dismal failures.

The purpose of this diagnostic service is to shift attention from information technology to the effectiveness of the executives who manage it. The discovery of the business value of computers lies in their linking with the business plans. Computers on which you run information systems can deliver productivity gains if they are explicitly connected to overcoming existing business problems and supporting competitive objectives. In isolation, they are just pieces of metal, plastic, or glass. The contributions of information technologies to increasing the *Management Value-added* ratio to *Management Costs*, that is *Management Productivity*, will tell you if computers produce a business payoff.

Measuring Management Productivity is the key to knowing how to invest in information technologies. Correctly diagnose conditions that will improve *Management Productivity* before you resystemize, reengineer, or automate. Make management more productive, by electronic means, if you know where, when, and how. Automate the business processes that are directly linked to the success of the business.

The *Management Productivity* diagnostic practice has its origins in studies [Strassmann, *The Business Value of Computers*] that questioned why the relationship between profitability and computer spending appeared to be random:

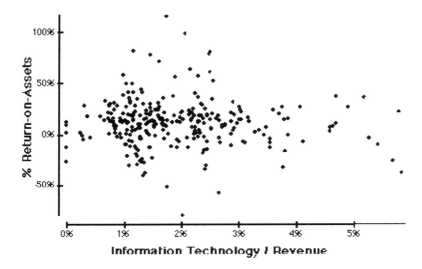

The lack of correlation between information technology spending and profitability is contrary to advertised claims. It defies the common belief that investing in electronic processing of information somehow leads to lower costs and results in competitive advantage.

Should these findings create doubt about the rapidly rising computer budgets of the last thirty years? Without good answers as to how to validate their gains, corporate executives kept voting with their checkbooks to automate their activities on a scale that exceeded anything in history in scope and speed. Computer budgets increased faster than purchases for any other class of equipment and now exceed the profits for half of the firms that employ them. Failing firms did not lag behind superior firms in the rush to install the best and latest computing equipment. There are unprofitable companies that spend more money on computers than similar firms that realize large profits. Does that signify that the decision to purchase information technology is unrelated to results? Research, on which this diagnostic method is based, suggests that corporate over-achievers differ from underachievers. They also manage their computers differently.

Conventional financial ratios are unsatisfactory for measuring the benefits of information systems. Companies competing in equivalent markets, with a similar capital structure, comparable production technologies, and the same computer models, can deliver remarkably different financial results. This diversity is attributable not to computers but to Management Value-added. Since the management of information is inseparable from management's general roles, we view the processing of information by electronic circuitry as an extension of traditional management roles by other means. This diagnostic methodology is addressed to those executives who are trying to extract business value from their investments in computers. After applying it, clients should have greater confidence in deploying information technologies in assisting their organization in achieving its goals.

About Measurement

Goal-Setting and Measurement

Misapplications of technology occur when goals and actions are confused. Organizations launch projects for "giving personal computers to all salespersons," "automating clerical labor," "converting from batch-processing to online systems," "introducing artificial intelligence into decision support applications," or engaging in the building of an "executive information system." By not separating the validity of goals from the implementation, the conflicts between ends and means will confuse even the best-intended schemes.

The problem is that complete goal-validation, such as a detailed commitment to getting specific benefits, is a painful process. The appraisal of a particular goal is possible only if the goal is clear, measurable, and supported by verifiable cases. Most importantly, verifiable goals specify how we will measure the result of our efforts after we complete the intended project.

Coming up with proof that the desired goals were reached is a tough assignment. That is hard to do, especially if the proposed technology project needs support from constituencies who have conflicting needs, opposing interests, and diverse qualifications in considering the merits of the proposal. In the public sector, such projects are carried by contention between competing agencies. In the business world, they are compromises arising from the annual budget process which favors the dressing up of goals into acceptable projects. Unless an information technology has measurable financial outcomes, the clarity of its goals is questionable.

When you introduce computers into an organization, their effects are systemic, affecting the working of the whole company. The consequences will modify the way the firm operates. Because of this, measurements must reflect the aftereffects of many changes, instead of just one isolated improvement. It is relatively easy to achieve simple goals by sacrificing others. The effect of increasing market share will ripple through every department. Production, personnel, manufacturing, and distribution functions never will be the same. This raises the issue of goal-setting for information technology investments: What principles help us examine a proposal for changing systems that manage an organization? The answer is that you should measure the *productivity* of organizations before and after automation. Gains in organizational productivity would tell us if the new system improved overall performance, because the overall advantages outweigh the overall disadvantages. What then is the meaning of organizational *productivity* in an information-based company?

The Productivity of Information Systems

The term *productivity* is about two hundred years old. At the start of the industrial revolution, factory owners needed a quick way to assess operating results without having to wait for financial reports. Productivity was output divided by input. For example, if a blast furnace produced ten tons of steel per worker, and next year the same furnace produced eleven tons of steel per worker, labor productivity increased by 10 percent.

Physical Measures of Productivity

Under the influence of Frederick Taylor, the measurement of efficiency and productivity came to the factory floor. Productivity was redefined as the physical *output* produced with a given number of physical *inputs*. For example, the number of shafts, bearings, or carburetors produced per work-hour or man-week would be a measure of direct labor productivity. The whole idea of physical productivity also applied to national economic measurements. Today, U.S. productivity is a weighted mix of physical outputs (tons of steel or paper, kilowatts of electricity, etc.) divided by a weighted mix of labor inputs, such as hours worked. In addition, national productivity includes an allowance for capital inputs, such as the reported financial value of physical assets. This measurement of productivity was satisfactory when the country's main economic activities were agriculture or manufacturing and when physical outputs were comparable to similar physical inputs at an earlier time. A bushel of wheat or a ton of pig iron did not change much over the period when comparing productivity results.

During the 1930s, quality began to displace quantity as a critical factor in advanced industrial economies. As a result, imperfections in the measurement of productivity started creeping in. Automobiles and convenience foods sold in 1960 or 1970 were not equivalent to those produced in the 1930s or 1940s. The labor-intensive assembly lines of the pre-World War II factories were not comparable to the highly engineered production processes thirty years later. Accurately measuring gains for the number of automobiles or tons of freeze-dried vegetables could not be done, because dissimilar outputs were produced with different inputs. Similarly, a computer in 1989 is not comparable with a computer in 1979 or 1969, regardless of how we try to define their equivalence in millions of instructions per second per dollar.

Problems in Reporting on Physical Productivity

After 1970, serious difficulties in interpreting productivity numbers began to surface. In advanced industrial societies, the manufacturing sector declined as the origin of *Value-added* shifted from production (reported in the manufacturing sector) to distribution (reported in the service sector). When a steel company shifts its warehousing to a distributor, this appears as a loss to the production sector and a gain in the services sector.

The automation of a factory reduced the direct labor force, and therefore presumed to improve productivity. But for every factory worker displaced, there were now two other people employed in the company's offices. These changes appeared in corporate productivity calculations as gains in manufacturing productivity. The offsetting productivity declines from office work did not get reported, because no means were available for measuring the outputs of the rising office population. You had inputs (office costs) but no easily identifiable outputs. Without output estimates you cannot come up with useful measures of productivity.

Some banks and insurance companies have reorganized themselves on the model of paper work factories. They began measuring the productivity of clerical personnel using the principles of industrial management. Detroit time-and-motion study engineers found employment in New York offices when computers were introduced on a massive scale. The industrial engineers succeeded only in streamlining clerical labor. They failed in dealing with the rising costs of professional staffs which were excluded from productivity calculations because their output was intangible. The traditional formula for determining "productivity" as a critical business indicator was at a dead end. Nobody knew how to calculate the gains, if there were any, caused by the growing costs of information work. Without a generally accepted correct measure of productivity, you could not support massive investments in computers. The stage was set for the approaching decline in the seemingly unlimited appetite for more information technology.

Omission of Management from Productivity Measurement

The fastest rising and the most expensive labor costs—executives, managers, administrators, professionals, and officials—whom I designate as *Management*, were omitted from all productivity calculations. *Management* was overhead, with "intangible" and "immeasurable" physical results, and therefore had been exempt from the measurement of their outputs. "White collar" productivity studies concerned only the work products of clerical and secretarial personnel. It was acceptable to claim savings from reducing fully burdened clerical and secretarial labor hours, even if this added to the size of managerial and professional staffs.

The widespread adoption of computers made the misjudgments of productivity only worse. Computers generated outputs for which internal customers often did not pay. Computers also supported people delivering intangible advice to *Management*, whose output also was intangible. This meant that the economy began absorbing large quantities of information-processing capital unrelated to the generation of profits. Legions of specialists attending to the needs of overhead personnel joined the payroll. Productivity was no longer the traditional concept of a ratio of physical *outputs* to *inputs*. *Output* was indeterminate and *input* was an untraceable overhead expense.

The first twenty years of euphoric acceptance of computers ended when overhead costs (including supporting capital) surpassed direct labor costs (including their supporting capital) in the service sector. Since the immeasurable became the largest *input*, physical productivity ratios ceased to have any meaning.

Financial Measures from the Industrial Era

Because there were no valid measures of productivity, investments in computers were justified only in strictly financial terms. Corporate procedure was already familiar with filling out similar forms for the approval of fork-lift trucks, the building of warehouses, and the buying of a new milling machine. Forms for acquiring information systems also took on the same appearance. These forms are much alike, regardless of the industry or the country. They differ only in detail as to calculating and documenting *ROA* (return on assets) or *ROI* (return on investment).

Every method for computing *ROA* or *ROI* goes back to the eighteenth century, when capital was the most important element in organizing the industrial means for production. According to this view, all profits created by a company are possible because of capital. Labor was a commodity. *Management* was overhead to the costs of labor. Therefore, *ROA* and *ROI* are the essence of free-market as well as planned economies, for they calculate the efficiency with which you use capital. Following this outlook, the financial analysts, the stock market, and your shareholders will judge you primarily by your capital efficiency and not by the efficiency of how you utilize your human resources.

To come up with the financial measure of productivity is simple: you divide profit (the final output of any enterprise) by capital (the decisive input to any enterprise). Labor, management, land, and material inputs are bought at commodity prices. What counts then, is capital. If capital is well invested, you get productivity. This explains why management theorists until now have been primarily concerned with the efficiency of using capital. That was acceptable prior to the introduction of huge administrative staffs. Management's concentration on capital budgeting was essential. The capacity to manage capital resources meant having access to more capital for large plants to produce steel, refine oil, generate electricity, and make appliances. An adequate supply of inexpensive capital was a prerequisite for gaining market share through production and distribution efficiencies. The fascination with the acquisition and management of capital obscured the understanding that the annual costs of corporate bureaucracies were becoming more expensive than the annual carrying charges for capital assets.

The Project Authorization Bias

The concentration on capital investment changed the ways of managing innovation. Management focused on capital budgeting as the place where they could exercise maximum influence over the future directions of a business. Once a capital investment was approved, the operating expense would then follow from the initial investment decision. Therefore, the annual costs would not be amenable to major changes. As a consequence of such thinking, all innovation required estimation of expected benefits and costs with reasonable confidence

When such investment-oriented logic was applied to computer projects, it resulted in elaborate, lengthy, and tortuous approval procedures. In the absence of reliable productivity measures, industrial-age executives became convinced that the preferred way to control computers was through project authorization procedures which reduced the risks of computerization to a minimum. This resulted in favoring projects that automated existing business procedures instead of changing them to take advantage of the new information-handling methods. Investment-oriented executives failed to recognize that computerization is an incremental, continuous, and evolutionary organizational learning process that requires better controls over operating results for the entire business. Cumbersome project review procedures produced elongated development schedules, and created a tendency to combine long overdue incremental improvements into a single costly project. Emphasis on controlling new investments led to the establishment of the information system as a discrete and separate function, instead of integrating it into every manager's job.

Executives who rely primarily on project authorizations to control computer spending are focusing on a diminishing fraction of total costs. As soon as the annual growth rate in information technology spending slows down below 10 percent, less than 20 percent of the total budget would be available for new development. The rest of the budget goes for ongoing maintenance and inflationary salary increases. The share of capital expenses for any new information technology development is also very small, because most of the cost of installing new applications is in systems analysis, coordination, and training. Relying on project authorizations of information technology hardware investments as the principal method to guide the application of computers becomes irrelevant.

Post-Industrial Development

By 1980, global competition created excess production capacity for nearly every product or service. Rapidly accumulating profits were seeking out opportunities for reinvestment. The globalization of financial markets created conditions where capital became a readily traded commodity, not a scarce resource. Hundreds of billions of dollars moved electronically, at a moment's notice, from country to country whenever there was a small change in the price of capital. When international financial transactions exceeded international trade by a multiple of twenty or more, finance capital ceased to be the prime explanation for value creation. Capital was now a commodity, like everything else.

The scarce resources today are people who can organize and motivate the productive capacities of their employees, and who know how to maximize the use of capital. The scarce resource of the post-industrial world is *Management*. If a company is profitable, it is because of *Management*, and not because of capital. One can determine *Management* costs by first identifying all *Operations* costs, which are the essential resources for serving today's customers. Everything not in *Operations* is, by definition, *Management*:

Operations	**Management**
• How to do	• How to organize
• Doing the things right	• Doing the right things
• Today's business	• Tomorrow's business
• Structured tasks	• Unstructured tasks
• Today's decisions for today	• Today's decisions for future
• Workflow shapes decisions	• Decisions shape workflow

The Characteristics of Operations and Management

Companies in the same industry, with the same technology and same capital structure, can have widely differing profits. Research has found that high capital intensity is always harmful to profitability. Therefore, measuring business productivity only by means of capital productivity ratios will not reflect the real causes for generating profits.

The modern enterprise employs large numbers of computer-supported managers. Measuring its capital productivity will not tell us much about this critical resource. Measuring the productivity of its direct labor is also insufficient. Reporting automobiles produced per worker per year does not tell us much about what cars are being produced with robots. Boasting about gains in clerical productivity will be equally misleading. If management is the scarce resource, and if management is the key to the productivity of organizations, why not measure "management productivity" instead of "capital" or "labor" productivity? This approach would be different from the way today's economists or accountants think about evaluating business results. Most importantly, measuring *Management productivity* would open the way to exploring the benefits of computers used by their principal customers, the managers of information.

Measuring Management Productivity

The measurement of organizational productivity is possible only if we consider how well a firm's leadership guides the business so that the employees' contributions remain constructive. How well management manages, over an extended period of time, is the aim of measuring *Management productivity*. From a shareholder's standpoint, management—not capital—should be the investment that needs watching. The only evaluations that make sense concern the effectiveness of management. *Management productivity* answers the following question: For every dollar spent on management, how many dollars of net gain accrue to the shareholders?

Computers primarily serve management and control purposes. Because the use of information technology is not evenly distributed among workers, we can get a better understanding of its effectiveness by separating its managerial uses from other applications. We can then evaluate the effectiveness of *Management* with or without computers. We can also isolate cases showing superior managerial productivity, and then examine their characteristics of computer use that differ from cases that show inferior managerial productivity.

Research extending over a period of ten years led to the concept of *Return-On-Management (tm)*. This ratio does a good job not only in evaluating information technology, but also in identifying excessive overhead costs. This ratio is calculated by first isolating the *Management Value-added* of a company, and then dividing it by the company's total *Management Costs:*

Return-On-Management(tm) = F(Management Value-added, Management Costs)

Management Value-added is that which remains after every contributor to a firm's inputs gets paid. If *Management Value-added* is greater than Management Costs, you can say that managerial efforts are productive because the managerial *outputs* exceed managerial inputs.

Another way of looking at the Return-on-Management ratio (R-O-M(tm) Productivity Index) is to view it as a measure of productivity. It answers the question of how many surplus dollars you get for every dollar paid for Management.

R-O-M(tm) Index = F(Management Output, Management Input) = Management Productivity

To attribute all surplus value to *Management*, instead of capital or labor, is a departure from classic economics. It is *Management* that makes the investment and pricing decisions. It is *Management* that motivates the employees. It is *Management* that chooses products and markets. It is *Management* that organizes the suppliers and the production and delivery of goods to customers. Good *Management* can get more of the capital it needs, at a lower interest, than poor *Management*.

The scarce resource of contemporary society is not capital or technology, but *Management*. The time has come to begin measuring it explicitly. *Management Productivity* is not apparent from capital-based financial ratios that only tell us about *Management* by proxy. The theory behind this concept comes from the idea that information (e.g., *Management*) is a disorder-defying phenomenon which assures the survival of a firm in a competitive environment. Without the continuous intervention by *Management,* every enterprise must perish from chaotic conditions which arise when external information (about customers and competitors) and internal information fail to guide people in what to do. When that happens, people cannot cooperate in bringing in new revenues.

According to laws of thermodynamics, machines always produce less energy than they consume. *Management* has the capacity to construct a device—an organization—that extracts from a hostile environment *Net Value-added* (*Outputs*) in excess of total costs (*Inputs*). A well-managed organization is superior to any engine ever invented. A profitable corporation generates a net surplus of wealth. For effective organizations, *Output* always exceeds *Input*, which defies the law of physics that states that this is impossible and disorder must ultimately prevail. Our civilization has created an enormous accumulation of wealth, because *Management* has learned how to increase cooperation through organization of its productive resources.

How to measure a phenomenon that must generate a positive *Net Value-added in order* to survive is central to the issue of what *Management* is all about. For the last two hundred years, management was evaluated by its capacity to extract new surplus (profits) out of past accumulations of profits (invested capital). Since smart management can get all the capital it can use, the old formulation can now be replaced by directly measuring the productivity of *Management* as an information-processing function. We measure the *Output/Input* ratio by finding what's left after *Management* pays everyone, and dividing that by the costs of managing the Net Value-added creation process. This is why it is critical to find how much information (*Management*) is necessary to run an enterprise.

Companies that can extract more *Net Value-added* from the marketplace, while consuming less information to accomplish this feat, will be the winners. The question of what is information effectiveness is resolved by finding how much *Net Value-added* can be created with the smallest combination of managers and computers. *Measuring Management Value-added* is then the key to evaluating organizational performance and to measuring the effects of computers on management information systems.

Finding Management Value-Added

Finding the *Management Value-added* is similar to extracting gold from rocks or river sand. First, you sift out large pieces of matter that clearly do not belong. After that, you do not assume that whatever is left is gold because there is still too much extraneous matter. You concentrate on removing foreign material, making sure that in the process you do not accidentally discard anything that is valuable.

Management Value-added is the purified residue of a winnowing process. You obtain it if you have exercised care in removing all variables that do not belong.

Adjusting for Purchases

As the first step in the cost-separation process, remove from *Revenues* the costs of *Purchased Raw and Finished Materials, Parts, Energy, and Services*. These essential inputs are managed by someone other than the firm's management. Their prices already reflect the suppliers' management costs.

Next, subtract the cost of *Interest*. Interest payments are just like payments for any other service. In this case, the supplier is usually a bank. Effective management will pay less for loans than an unreliable one. What matters is the incremental *Value-added* that management creates with loans. In this respect, the money that management obtains is not different than any other rental contract for equipment or services.

Next, subtract all *Taxes*. Profit after taxes is the indicator that matters to the shareholder. Subtract taxes directly from revenues—before, not after other expenditures—because government makes sure it gets paid before anybody else. In this way, taxes become payments to the most insistent supplier. All taxes are then an *involuntary purchase*. Allocation from headquarters is also a form of imposed taxation and must be subtracted from *Revenue*. What remains is the *Business Value-added*.

It is revealing to examine the enormous range in *Business Value-added* as a percentage of *Revenue* for manufacturing firms:

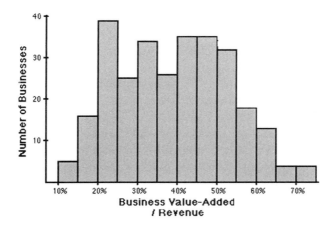

In our analyses, all productivity evaluations will be based on *Business Value-added* instead of on *Revenue*, because companies with a high degree of vertical integration (a high *Business Value-added/Revenue* ratio) can justify more *Management* than those with a lower level of integration. Productive executives are likelier to make better choices on the mix of what to buy and what to make. They can then support the additional costs of coordination and integration, provided that the incremental value-added is greater than its incremental costs.

Superior management can also get better prices for their purchases. This translates into improved *Business Value-added*. Choosing efficient suppliers, especially in manufacturing, offers the greatest possible opportunities for profit improvement because purchases will be the largest cost element. *Value-added* analysis becomes the key to judging the worth of computer investments that support buying activities.

Focusing on *Business Value-added* gives an unobstructed view of the scope of a firm's managerial activities. It is unfortunate that accounting practices fold an indistinguishable mixture of direct labor, production overhead, and purchases into the cost-of-goods, htereby making it hard to tell whether the company is increasing or decreasing value-added. For value-added analysis, you must first extricate external purchases from the cost ledgers. Clients accustomed to value-added concepts do not have these difficulties, because taxation rules dictate value-added financial reporting as a matter of routine.

Adjusting for Shareholder Value-Added

After paying suppliers for their share of inputs, *Management* has to account for the shareholders' value-added. The major distortion in the *Return-On-Asset* calculations is that ROA for low-debt businesses will be higher when compared with high-debt businesses. Calculating the *R-O-M(tm)* Index adjusts such comparisons by subtracting from the *Business Value-added* the going rate of the costs of shareholder capital, multiplied by the market (or book) value of shareholder equity. This calculation is Identical to the current approach of calculating the cost of capital for the Economic Value added (EVA).

Subtracting the going rate of shareholder capital costs from after-tax profits is another way of computing the economic "rent" for capital. It is also known as the "economic profit" of a firm, which is different from the usually quoted number known as "operating profit." According to this view, shareholders' economic profit, or economic rent, is equal to operating profits minus interest costs, minus the investment revenues a company's assets could earn if employed elsewhere. Such rent can also be calculated by estimating the breakup value of a firm, and multiplying that with an interest rate that can be earned in a comparable investment.

Regardless of the technique used for computing the shareholder *Value-added*, it is essential that it reduces reported accounting profits. Otherwise, the financial reports overstate the contributions by *Management* and could end up paying bonuses on *Value-added* which rightfully belongs to shareholders.

Adusting for Business Cost

Day-to-day *Operations* are paid for next. These include the fully burdened costs of employee payrolls, asset depreciation, and interest. Operations include everything that is essential for getting today's goods and services produced and delivered to today's customers.

Management Costs are calculated by considering that everything that's not in Operations is automatically placed in this category. The *Management Value-added* is *Revenue* minus *Purchases* minus *Shareholder Value-added* minus the *Costs of Operations* minus the *Costs of Management*.

The following diagram should help in understanding cost elements for deriving the Management Value-added:

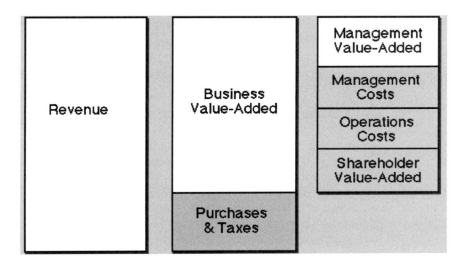

In favorable cases, the *Management Value-added* can be a large multiple of *Management Costs*. There are firms where for every dollar paid to Management, two or more dollars of surplus *Management Value-added* are created. The unhappy aspect of *Management Value-added* is that it can be less than zero. Over 20 percent of firms showed a negative *Management Value-added*, although more than 50 percent of those still report profits and a positive R-O-A, using generally accepted accounting principles.

Computing R-O-M®

Data-gathering begins the process for computing standard performance indicators. Each of these indicators has been tested to give statistically valid correlations about the relationship between the structure of management costs and business profitability. The first part is an outgrowth of empirical work done since the early 1970s at the General Electric Company, the Strategic Planning Institute (PIMS), and now continuing at the MANTIS (Management Tools and Information Services, Inc.) research consortium.

Part 1, *Critical Characteristics*, is identical to the short form of strategic analysis as used by the MANTIS organization as a Strategic Business Analysis report. Clients may opt to fill out a more elaborate questionnaire to get more diagnostic indicators to deal with matters of marketing strategy.

Part 2, *Management Productivity Characteristics*, will collect data needed to compute the value of R-O-M(tm) and to come up with insights about the effectiveness of overhead expenses.

Clients may also wish to apply R-O-M(tm) techniques in analyzing major investment proposals involving information technologies. A *Functional Economic Analysis* package and a risk-analysis service is also available.

R-O-M® Diagnosis

The aim of the *Return-On-Management* diagnostic process is to imitate practices well established in confidential medical testing. The findings will not produce specific action recommendations. It is not feasible to take historical statistics and generate a specific prescription for what to do from that information. The goal is to offer well-researched ratios which compare a client's actual business characteristics against a range found in comparable organizations. The goal is diagnose those distinctions that suggest what may be detracting from the capacity of a business to reach its profit potential.

In sound medical practice, clinical testing always precedes the prescription of a specific therapy. The same approach applies in dealing with managerial pathologies. Information technology should not be examined as a machine tool, but as a pharmaceutical. With proper diagnosis, the right timing, and the correct dosage, pharmaceuticals can produce miraculous results. If applied incorrectly, they can kill you.

Collection of Standard Data

To get comparable data across a range of industries and in different countries, all data definitions are standardized. Most of the information called for in filling out these forms is routinely available from existing accounting data and from marketing research sources.

The R-O-M(tm) data form requires splitting costs for *creating* the customer value-added from costs incurred in *supporting* the delivery of products and of services. The forms also instruct how to allocate information technology costs to business functions. To document how the original accounting data is distributed, create a spreadsheet which tracks all changes.

When a client experiments with R-O-M, it is sometimes possible to take a few short cuts. For some industries, I have enough purchase-to-revenue ratios that my computer can estimate the likeliest total value-added. If this approximation turns out to be important, I will ask for the actual purchase costs.

Though the data-gathering forms should be self-explanatory, analysts will need help in interpreting some data definitions. They also may have difficulties in discerning what is the called for accuracy of a few nonaccounting numbers. Clients have direct access to me either by facsimile, telex, or electronic mail to resolve any questions without much delay.

Comparison against a Data Base

From looking at many case studies we have identified correlations between the R-O-M(tm) measure of productivity and *critical performance ratios*. Some of these insights come from research that has its origins in the PIMS studies about business strategy. Studies dealing with the relationship between overhead costs and information technology are derived from work done under PIMS auspices (the MPIT project), and from client engagements.

After receipt of the finished management productivity forms, the data will be compared with the data base for a data-consistency check. Out-of-limit conditions are identified and the client is contacted to find out whether the deviant information should be included in the diagnosis. *Critical performance ratios* are then calculated from the accepted data and results compared with information in the R-O-M(tm) and MANTIS data bases as well as against constantly updated research findings. Great care is taken to assure statistically reliable comparisons. To that end we recognize differences by industries (by major standard industry classification categories), geographic location (U.S.A. and Canada vs. Europe), taxation, capital structure (the debt/equity ratio), and costs of equity capital.

If a client's case is unique, I shall refund half of the fee and the client will be mailed a comprehensive report showing why he is incomparable.

The entire diagnostic method relies on annual *critical performance ratios,* therefore, the results are indifferent to changes in currency or inflation. When the annual data contain unusual one-time costs, such as in the case of atypical marketing programs, a discounted cash flow model will compute equivalent annual costs.

For large multidivisional companies, comparisons can be made against both the general data base and a customized data base if there is a large enough sample to make the additional analyses statistically significant.

Secutity

The extreme sensitivity of the input data and of the diagnostic results calls for precautions equivalent to the handling of classified military information. The following practices safeguard the client's data:

- The client will be given a randomly chosen block of identification numbers. After that, all forms, communications, and final reports carry only that number. If a client makes an unintentional disclosure, all the compromised information will be returned and resubmitted in a different format.

- Clients may wish to disguise costs by multiplying or dividing every number by a constant. For instance, Swedish data can be converted into Italian liras.

- Clients should submit their data forms through a third party to prevent accidental disclosures. This procedure works well when the data gathering and diagnostic interpretation is done by third parties, such as a trade association or the corporate staff of a multidivisional company.

- All forms, final reports, and interim communications are transmitted by registered mail. Facsimile transmissions of data need verbal authentication at both ends.

We are following the same rules as on the PIMS project, where detailed financial information about more than 2,000 businesses was accumulated over twenty years without compromising security.

Strategic Business Report

The first thirteen forms in the *Management Productivity* collection assemble the key descriptors about the competitive health and the financial fundamentals of a business.

Where accurate numbers are available, it is preferred that they be used on line items in the financial statement. Where no accurate numbers are available, for example, the competitors' market share or product quality, the best estimates by knowledgeable observers are enough. Where even estimates are difficult to make, a neutral answer is better than no answer. The chances are that many estimates may not influence the diagnostic findings. If the neutral answer appears as an important difference, then more effort is required to find out the right descriptor.

Usually, it will take about three hours per *Strategic Business Unit* (SBU) to complete the forms with adequate precision to check out the adequacy of the information. In filling out the forms, a few rules are in order:

- The form should be finished for each *Strategic Business Unit* in a company. An SBU is defined as a coherent strategic entity (i.e., a well-defined product line going to a well-defined market). It may or may not follow the lines of a divisional organization. It may share factories or marketing resources with other SBUs. If in doubt about how many SBUs should be recognized, choose the smaller number.

- Where accounts need to be allocated to the various SBUs, a simple formula is always preferred to a complex allocation scheme. The moderate differences that may be produced by more complicated formulas usually have little effect on strategic diagnosis.

- Usually, the allocation of assets, joint production equipment, or joint costs across SBUs can be done on the basis of value-added. Allocations based on revenue should be avoided unless there is defensible logic behind such an approach. All support costs—and this applies especially to research, engineering, systems support, and programming maintenance—should be allocated using estimates of the resources consumed and not using unrelated ratios, such as employee headcount or assets.

- Market-related questions must focus on the *served market* of the SBU. The served market is that segment of the potential total market in which the business is an active competitor. This means that the business has a competitive product and makes an identifiable marketing effort. The relative ranking of the business and its competitors (as defined by market shares, relative prices, innovation, and relative quality) must be judged with reference to a well-defined *served market*. I find that this part of the diagnostic form gives the greatest problems to my clients, because the tend to forget the distinctions between what is the *total* market and what parts they are participating in.

The first thirteen data forms supply information that *generates the Strategic Business Report,* which is designed to monitor the competitive health and future financial prospects of the business. This diagnostic report is based on extensive empirical research of businesses with similar strategic characteristics.

The S*trategic Business Report* represents the simplest level of analysis. It is designed as a communication tool for the CEO, CFO, and the business management team. Its purpose is to identify where priorities should be placed and where information technology investments should be focused.

Management Productivity Report

These forms assemble the variables needed to do Return-on-Management diagnosis. As a rule, accounting precision of the information is unnecessary until further analysis shows that a data element is critically important.

Employment Characteristics

Organizational Complexity is an indicator of the information required for internal and external communications. Internal complexity is measured by counting communication layers between the chief executive and the first level of supervision. When counting, the layers include the starting level (e.g. CEO) and the recipient's level.

External complexity is measured by counting the layers from the chief executive to the customer who ultimately consumes the product or service. If a business passes goods unchanged through distributors and then through retailers to a consumer, then the layers between the consumer and the CEO must also be counted. If, however, the distributor incorporates the product as a component within another product, then only the layers dealing with the distributor should be counted.

Workstations are an indicator of the extent to which a business depends on electronic means for communications.

Working Hours are reported to make comparisons where different levels of productivity are shown because of different work practices.

The Employment Additions are used to calculate employee turnover rates. This is an indicator of the accumulated knowledge of a workforce.

The Management or Operations Categories

This distinction is the key to coming up with the measure of management productivity. The underlying concept here is that all costs essential for delivery of today's goods and services are classified as *Operations*. Everything else is automatically defined as *Management*. The *Management* function supplies the necessary support so that *Operations* can deliver today's output to today's customers. The *Management* function also acts today so that *Operations* can deliver tomorrow's output to tomorrow's customers.

In this way of thinking, *Management*, not *Operations* is the engine that drives the future profitability in the same way that today's profitability is the result of yesterday's management efforts.

Management, not Operations:

- Decides how to apportion revenue between suppliers, employees, shareholders, and debt-holders.

- Allocates money between today's problems and tomorrow's opportunities.

- Chooses and motivates employees. These are the paramount choices that make the difference in whether a firm ultimately prospers or declines.

- Chooses what markets to compete in, what prices to charge, and what prices to pay for wages, salaries, or purchases.

Management is the critical ingredient which makes the difference in delivering sustainable profits. A standard definition of the total costs of *Management* is a prerequisite for computing a comparable measure of management productivity.

Employment Table

Classifying personnel into the *Management* or *Operations* categories will probably involve more discussion than any of the other forms.

Never start with an estimate of how many employees are involved in *Management*. Care should be taken to first identify only *Operations*. These are employees who can be directly, and without much controversy, associated with producing revenues. For instance, the hours used in machining, in assembly parts, in taking telephone orders, in client billable time by a lawyer, etc., are clearly cases where *Direct Operations* personnel are involved.

The full-time equivalent number of employees is computed by taking direct hours and dividing them by the net working hours as defined in the Working Hours characteristics. For instance, a factory operator delivering 1550 direct working hours per year (e.g., 1550 hours divided by 37.5 hours/week * 52 weeks less 6 weeks for vacation, paid holidays, and absenteeism) would count as an equivalent 0.9 employee for *Direct Operations*. If the remaining 175 hours are spent in training and meeting attendance, an equivalent 0.1 employees should be entered as *Management*.

If a consultant bills only 50 percent of his net available time (the remainder expended in training, marketing support, and recruiting), then only 0.5 equivalent employees would be identified as *Direct Operations*. 0.5 equivalent employees would be entered as *Management*.

Do not classify all support functions as *Management*. For instance the transportation dispatcher in a warehouse would be classified as *Indirect Operations* if his functions are essential for the goods to move out. Because the physical transportation adds to the value the customer is paying for, you can classify the actual time the transportation dispatcher spends in dispatching goods as *Indirect Operations*.

A billing clerk that checks on whether the quantities on the loading dock correspond to the warehouse pick-list should be classified as *Management*, since checking for errors in warehouses, is an avoidable managerial procedure. The billing clerk's time spent in checking for errors adds little value to what the customer is willing to pay for. In classifying personnel, I take the position that all expenses for control, coordination, error checking, training, meetings, and supervision are results of imperfections in *Management* processes and should be recognized.

Production equipment maintenance and computer operations personnel (in a commercial service bureau) who are essential for the production and services to continue without interruption, would also be part of *Indirect Operations*.

As a rule, if an individual is essential for the delivery of a revenue-producing product or service, the time spent on such efforts should be classified as *Operations*. If a job is dictated by internal needs, such as innovation, product development, market research, materials testing, accounting, personnel, and advertising, then the person should be identified as *Management* because it is the purpose of management to take care of activities that will ensure the future of the enterprise. Special care should be taken to identify the large percentages of time expended by personnel, ordinarily viewed as *Direct* or *Indirect Operations* on managerial tasks such as meetings and training.

Proceed in filling out the Employment Table form by first identifying all full-time equivalent *Operations* personnel. The balance falls automatically into the *Management* headcount.

Remember: If you are not in *Operations*, then you are in *Management*.

Cost Structure Tables

Purchases should include goods and services supplied by suppliers. This also includes goods and services received from other divisions of the same company, if the purchases are made at competitive prices. Otherwise, all noncompetitive internal procurement should be in *Corporate Allocations*, at an estimated market price. Classifying *Labor Costs* should follow the rules outlined in filling out the *Employment Table*.

Attributing nonlabor costs to *Management* is handled in the *Management Support Costs* schedule. The simplest approach in computing this allocation is to first estimate the percent of *Management Cost* to *Total Labor Cost*. This number can then be corrected to allow for unusual costs, such as expenses for corporate headquarters, institutional advertising, pure research, and personnel development.

A separate schedule is supplied to identify the costs of *Information Technology*. Good records are usually available to show what fraction of total *Purchases*, *Labor*, and *Other Costs* are attributed to supporting *Information Technology*. The line item *Management Support* is intended to show what fraction of the total *Information Technology* expense is dedicated to *Management Functions*.

1993 Information Productivity(tm) Rankings, Industrial Companies

The following table is based on a combination of the 1993 Stern-Stewart Performance 1000 database, where Research and Development (R&D) as well as Sales, General & Administrative (S.G.&A.) expenses are likewise available from the 1993 Fortune 1000 database. The Information Productivity(tm) Index is a good approximation of the Management Productivity(tm) Index (R-O-M®), a ratio of Management Value-Added divided by the Costs of Management, as follows:

- Management Value-Added is precisely defined by the Economic Value-Added (EVA(tm)), as computed by Stern-Stewart. It uses the actual cost of capital for each company as well as a rigorous definition of the capital employed.

- Cost of Management is estimated by adding the expenses for R&D to the expenses for S.G.&A. The basis for this approximation is discussed elsewhere in the forthcoming book *Alignment of Information Management*, The Information Economics Press, 1995.

Click here for a more in-depth explanation of how to analyze Information Productivity(tm).

Click to return to the Strassmann, Inc. consulting page.

Rank	Company	R&D	SG&A	EVA	IP
Industry: Aerospace					
70	General Dynamics Corp.	0	2,878,000	398,000	0.14
168	Martin Marietta Corp.	0	8,647,224	398,000	0.03
183	Lockheed Corp.	0	12,227,000	289,000	0.02
195	Teleflex Inc.	0	140,965	2,000	0.01

232 Boeing [The] Co.	0	23,747,000	-332,000	-0.01
313 McDonnell Douglas Corp.	341,000	720,000	-110,000	-0.10
319 GenCorp Inc.	0	168,000	-19,000	-0.11
365 United Technologies Corp.	1,137,000	2,547,000	-666,000	-0.18
431 Sundstrand Corp.	0	291,900	-103,000	-0.35
473 Sequa Corp.	0	272,145	-167,000	-0.65
516 Thiokol Corp.	15,700	70,200	-91,000	-1.06
540 Rohr Inc.	0	43,800	-113,000	-2.58

Industry: Airlines

89 Southwest Airlines Co	0	382,048	34,000	0.09
332 UAL Corp.	0	4,447,000	-626,000	-0.14
367 Alaska Air Group Inc.	0	493,533	-93,000	-0.19
391 AMR Corp.	0	3,042,000	-738,000	-0.24
396 Delta Air Lines, Inc.	0	4,351,259	-1,147,000	-0.26
444 USAir Group, Inc.	0	1,539,494	-621,000	-0.40
545 Trans World Airlines, Inc.	0	78,202	-442,000	-5.65

Industry: Aluminum

525 Alumax Inc.	0	198,000	-292,000	-1.47
528 Maxxam Inc.	0	183,000	-296,000	-1.62
531 Aluminum Co. of America	130,400	603,600	-1,289,000	-1.76
536 Reynolds Metals Co.	0	371,600	-857,000	-2.31

Industry: Apparel

46 Warnaco Group Inc.	0	144,219	28,000	0.19
63 Nike, Inc.	0	922,261	151,000	0.16
69 Reebok International Ltd.	0	769,744	105,000	0.14
75 Fruit of the Loom, Inc.	0	240,100	31,000	0.13
182 VF Corp.	0	913,734	22,000	0.02
212 Liz Claiborne, Inc.	0	568,286	2,000	0.00
277 Kellwood Co.	0	143,771	-9,000	-0.06
410 Russell Corp.	0	185,107	-52,000	-0.28

Industry: Appliances & Furnish

36 Sunbeam-Oster Co., Inc.	0	124,154	33,000	0.27
45 Leggett & Platt, Inc.	0	192,400	41,000	0.21
142 Harman Int'l Industries	0	149,308	7,000	0.05
150 Kimball International, Inc.	0	160,192	6,000	0.04
181 La-Z-Boy Chair Co.	0	130,855	2,000	0.02
193 Circuit City Stores Inc.	0	744,650	7,000	0.01
276 Whirlpool Corp.	0	1,433,000	-83,000	-0.06
318 Masco Corp.	0	860,540	-93,000	-0.11
349 Tandy Corp.	0	1,354,676	-220,000	-0.16
357 Armstrong World Industries	0	505,000	-87,000	-0.17
376 Maytag Corp.	0	515,234	-101,000	-0.20

Industry: Auto Parts & Eqpmt

49 Standard Products Co.	20,971	49,768	13,000	0.18
120 Smith [A.O.] Corp.	0	96,345	7,000	0.07
151 Cummins Engine Co., Inc.	209,600	579,200	33,000	0.04
272 Echlin Inc.	0	420,460	-20,000	-0.05
273 Detroit Diesel Corp.	58,300	245,500	-15,000	-0.05
308 MascoTech, Inc.	0	179,680	-16,000	-0.09
327 Eaton Corp.	154,000	591,000	-91,000	-0.12
336 Dana Corp.	0	522,600	-74,000	-0.14
358 Federal-Mogul Corp.	0	227,300	-39,000	-0.17
487 Borg-Warner Automotive, Inc.	0	83,500	-61,000	-0.73

Industry: Beverages

34 Dr. Pepper/Seven-Up Cos.	0	393,300	110,000	0.28
41 Coca-Cola Co.	0	5,695,000	1,355,000	0.24
108 PepsiCo, Inc.	0	9,864,400	742,000	0.08
134 Universal Foods Corp.	0	196,102	12,000	0.06
141 Brown-Forman Corp.	0	846,517	39,000	0.05
231 Anheuser-Busch Companies	0	2,308,700	-20,000	-0.01
267 Coca-Cola Bottling Cons.	0	195,536	-10,000	-0.05
317 Coors [Adolph] Co.	13,008	818,911	-93,000	-0.11
380 Coca-Cola Enterprises Inc.	0	1,708,000	-358,000	-0.21

Industry: Broadcasting

21 CBS Inc.	0	461,300	180,000	0.39
170 Turner Broadcasting System	0	537,108	12,000	0.02
236 Capital Cities/ABC Inc.	0	1,097,826	-22,000	-0.02
333 Viacom Inc.	0	589,288	-83,000	-0.14
384 Tele-Communications, Inc.	0	1,425,000	-308,000	-0.22
480 Gaylord Entertainment Co.	0	73,800	-50,000	-0.68

Industry: Building Materials

6 USG Corp.	0	262,000	233,000	0.89
73 Valspar Corp.	24,579	102,750	16,000	0.13
93 Vulcan Materials Co.	0	116,072	11,000	0.09
122 RPM Inc.	0	181,255	10,000	0.06
202 York International Corp.	0	276,615	1,000	0.00
222 Sherwin-Williams Co.	0	981,268	-13,000	-0.01
262 Tecumseh Products Co.	0	78,400	-4,000	-0.05
282 Owens-Corning Fiberglass	69,000	338,000	-29,000	-0.07
362 PPG Industries, Inc.	201,200	871,700	-197,000	-0.18
486 Lafarge Corp.	0	161,449	-116,000	-0.72
509 Texas Industries Inc.	0	43,116	-44,000	-1.02

Industry: Business Machines & Services

56 Tech Data Corp.	0	79,390	13,000	0.16
64 Deluxe Corp.	0	570,504	79,000	0.14
77 HON Industries, Inc.	0	171,048	21,000	0.12
147 Reynolds and Reynolds Co.	0	227,502	10,000	0.04
153 Pitney Bowes Inc.	98,968	1,365,577	50,000	0.03
154 Diebold, Inc.	34,838	106,110	4,000	0.03
289 Standard Register [The] Co.	7,754	166,267	-14,000	-0.08
311 Miller [Herman], Inc.	24,513	230,219	-25,000	-0.10
459 Intelligent Electronics Inc.	0	52,477	-26,000	-0.5.

Industry: Cars & Trucks

15 Chrysler Corp.	0	3,377,000	1,628,000	0.48
110 PACCAR Inc.	0	331,200	27,000	0.08

331 Ford Motor Co.	0	9,687,000	-1,216,000	-0.13
476 Navistar International Corp.	94,000	305,000	-262,000	-0.66
477 General Motors Corp.	0	11,531,900	-7,593,000	-0.66

Industry: Chemicals

3 Georgia Gulf Corp.	0	38,901	46,000	1.18
11 Great Lakes Chemical Corp.	0	233,909	159,000	0.68
28 Int'l. Flavors & Fragrances	75,275	193,582	90,000	0.33
109 Nalco Chemical Co.	50,400	467,200	41,000	0.08
119 Betz Laboratories, Inc.	0	329,860	24,000	0.07
167 Morton International Inc.	68,600	391,700	12,000	0.03
270 Ferro Corp.	0	184,372	-9,000	-0.05
271 Ethyl Corp	75,624	272,760	-16,000	-0.05
300 Praxair Inc.	58,000	392,000	-38,000	-0.08
301 Dexter [The] Corp.	43,803	175,141	-17,000	-0.08
325 Lubrizol [The] Corp.	171,540	158,506	-40,000	-0.12
326 Air Products & Chemicals	92,300	744,000	-103,000	-0.12
364 Hercules Inc	76,121	371,725	-80,000	-0.18
381 Cabot Corp.	45,651	204,804	-53,000	-0.21
387 Rohm & Haas Co.	205,000	590,000	-171,000	-0.22
395 Engelhard Corp.	0	213,018	-54,000	-0.25
401 Du Pont [E.I.] De Nemours	1,493,000	8,732,000	-2,657,000	-0.26
402 Dow Chemical [The] Company	1,256,000	2,908,000	-1,093,000	-0.26
411 Grace [W.R.] & Co.	135,000	1,188,700	-365,000	-0.28
425 Monsanto Co.	695,000	1,747,000	-772,000	-0.32
429 Goodrich [B.F.] Co.	0	444,000	-149,000	-0.34
434 Witco Corp.	0	230,722	-84,000	-0.36
475 Wellman, Inc.	0	86,511	-57,000	-0.66
484 Lyondell Petrochemical Co.	0	130,000	-91,000	-0.70
488 Olin Corp.	41,000	300,000	-254,000	-0.74
493 Union Carbide Corp.	139,000	340,000	-379,000	-0.79
507 Geon [The] Company	0	51,100	-50,000	-0.98
533 IMC Fertilizer Group	0	60,400	-123,000	-2.04

Industry: Coal, Oil & Gas

14 MAPCO Inc.	0	72,800	37,000	0.51
96 Ultramar Corp.	0	477,094	44,000	0.09
175 Enron Oil & Gas Co.	75,743	1,255,041	33,000	0.02
260 Amoco Corp.	529,000	10,185,000	-467,000	-0.04
264 Mobil Corp.	405,000	20,980,000	-1,172,000	-0.05
265 Exxon Corp.	648,000	38,461,000	-1,801,000	-0.05
284 Unocal Corp.	164,000	1,440,000	-115,000	-0.07
295 Chevron Corp.	360,000	7,253,000	-629,000	-0.08
296 Burlington Resources Inc.	0	993,152	-82,000	-0.08
312 Total Petroleum [NA] Ltd.	0	418,400	-42,000	-0.10
322 Tosco Corp.	0	58,174	-7,000	-0.12
323 Coastal [The] Corp.	0	1,867,000	-216,000	-0.12
338 Ashland Oil, Inc.	0	1,715,620	-259,000	-0.15
344 Atlantic Richfield Co.	667,000	4,273,000	-797,000	-0.16
353 Sun Co., Inc.	22,000	2,671,000	-457,000	-0.17
373 Texaco Inc.	352,000	5,418,000	-1,126,000	-0.20
403 Quaker State Corp.	0	184,115	-50,000	-0.27
404 Pennzoil Co.	70,713	438,632	-135,000	-0.27
457 Mitchell Energy & Dev.	192,089	41,398	-115,000	-0.49
468 Phillips Petroleum Co.	256,000	880,000	-640,000	-0.56
482 Kerr-McGee Corp.	71,000	217,000	-201,000	-0.70
483 Diamond Shamrock R&M Inc.	0	97,600	-68,000	-0.70
490 Valero Energy Corp.	0	119,567	-91,000	-0.76
491 Murphy Oil Corp.	46,071	65,195	-86,000	-0.77
495 Maxus Energy Corp.	56,800	50,700	-88,000	-0.82
496 Louisiana Land & Exploration	48,800	73,700	-101,000	-0.82
502 FINA, Inc.	15,844	140,850	-139,000	-0.89
503 Amerada Hess Corp.	314,087	596,919	-809,000	-0.89
518 Occidental Petroleum Corp.	102,000	781,000	-962,000	-1.09
522 Union Texas Petroleum	93,640	23,780	-137,000	-1.17
530 Oryx Energy Co.	95,000	98,000	-321,000	-1.66

Industry: Computer Software & Services

5 Cisco Systems Inc.	44,254	130,682	166,000	0.95
17 Microsoft Corp	470,000	1,324,000	821,000	0.46

18 SynOptics Communications	65,754	175,693	100,000	0.41
38 Automatic Data Processing	132,386	617,194	188,000	0.25
103 Oracle Systems Corp.	146,420	792,736	78,000	0.08
171 Merisel Inc.	0	187,152	4,000	0.02
219 Computer Associates Int'l.	207,365	1,038,439	-10,000	-0.01
280 Computer Sciences Corp.	0	238,960	-17,000	-0.07
485 Comdisco, Inc.	0	197,000	-141,000	-0.72
513 First Data Corp.	0	194,666	-204,000	-1.05

Industry: Computers & Peripherals

4 Gateway 2000, Inc.	0	121,682	135,000	1.11
12 EMC Corp.	58,977	162,461	119,000	0.54
32 Quantum Corp.	63,019	110,934	51,000	0.29
76 Compaq Computer Corp.	169,000	913,000	128,000	0.12
113 Seagate Technology	154,005	222,071	25,000	0.07
146 Silicon Graphics Inc.	136,641	310,761	18,000	0.04
245 3Com Corp.	64,346	170,197	-7,000	-0.03
246 Apple Computer, Inc.	664,564	1,632,362	-64,000	-0.03
258 Sun Microsystems Inc.	445,356	1,104,498	-58,000	-0.04
288 Hewlett-Packard Co.	1,761,000	4,554,000	-497,000	-0.08
340 Dell Computer Corp.	42,358	267,982	-51,000	-0.16
369 Xerox Corp.	883,000	5,648,000	-1,267,000	-0.19
385 Unisys Corp.	515,200	1,648,900	-472,000	-0.22
406 Cray Research, Inc.	145,700	157,616	-85,000	-0.28
414 Internatl Business Machines	5,558,000	18,282,000	-6,797,000	-0.29
419 Digital Equipment Corp.	1,530,119	4,447,160	-1,842,000	-0.31
424 Western Digital Corp.	101,593	90,470	-61,000	-0.32
426 AST Research, Inc.	31,969	193,307	-74,000	-0.33
435 Storage Technology Corp.	163,286	399,595	-211,000	-0.37
441 Tandem Computers Inc.	313,298	847,047	-455,000	-0.39
445 Intergraph Corp.	160,294	342,513	-199,000	-0.40
464 Data General Corp.	100,172	346,740	-237,000	-0.53
504 Amdahl Corp.	334,514	354,939	-639,000	-0.93
512 Conner Peripherals Corp.	137,465	186,269	-336,000	-1.04

Industry: Conglomerates

22 Coltec Industries Inc.	0	192,437	73,000	0.38
163 Textron Inc.	0	2,586,400	80,000	0.03

164 Pall Corp.	40,036	262,598	9,000	0.03
165 General Electric Co.	0	14,761,000	418,000	0.03
166 Dial [The] Corp.	0	2,775,110	96,000	0.03
194 Whitman Corp.	0	582,300	8,000	0.01
213 TRW Inc.	378,000	707,000	-5,000	0.00
214 Tenneco Inc.	0	3,504,000	14,000	0.00
215 Rockwell International Corp.	0	1,374,200	4,000	0.00
255 Premark International Inc.	0	1,236,600	-36,000	-0.03
261 Alco Standard Corp.	0	1,378,814	-60,000	-0.04
268 Teledyne, Inc.	0	466,400	-22,000	-0.05
269 Ogden Corp.	0	942,359	-44,000	-0.05
299 Allied-Signal Inc.	0	1,338,000	-113,000	-0.08
350 Harcourt General, Inc.	0	1,131,944	-177,000	-0.16
447 ITEL Corp.	0	431,600	-181,000	-0.42
505 Figgie International Inc.	0	166,487	-156,000	-0.94
514 Valhi, Inc.	0	113,107	-119,000	-1.05

Industry: Construction & Engineering Services

81 EG&G, Inc.	0	113,107	26,000	0.11
448 Foster Wheeler Corp.	0	204,049	-87,000	-0.43
479 McDermott International	0	147,321	-99,000	-0.67
494 Morrison Knudsen Corp.	3,701	37,358	-33,000	-0.80
534 Fluor Corp.	0	43,682	-92,000	-2.11

Industry: Containers - Glass, Metal, Plastic

16 Crown Cork & Seal Co.	0	126,600	60,000	0.47
463 Ball Corp.	0	179,100	-94,000	-0.52
506 Owens-Illinois, Inc.	42,300	182,900	-217,000	-0.96

Industry: Discount & Fashion Retail

60 Gap [The], Inc.	0	748,193	118,000	0.16
85 May Department [The] Stores	0	2,196,000	251,000	0.11
87 Wal-Mart Stores, Inc.	0	10,333,218	1,056,000	0.10
88 TJX Companies, Inc.	0	674,055	66,000	0.10
106 Toys R Us Inc.	0	1,497,011	123,000	0.08
107 Service Merchandise Co.	0	673,744	53,000	0.08
132 Home Depot [The], Inc.	0	1,846,690	114,000	0.06

139 Melville Corp.	0	2,956,081	134,000	0.05
179 Penney [J.C.] Co.	0	4,508,000	99,000	0.02
192 Dillard Department Stores	0	1,239,049	15,000	0.01
210 Limited [The], Inc.	0	1,259,896	2,000	0.00
229 Lowe's Companies, Inc.	0	746,279	-9,000	-0.01
239 Payless Cashways, Inc.	0	570,016	-14,000	-0.02
240 Meyer [Fred], Inc.	0	761,627	-16,000	-0.02
253 Dayton-Hudson Corp.	0	3,518,000	-105,000	-0.03
285 Nordstrom, Inc.	0	940,579	-65,000	-0.07
315 US Shoe Corp1	0	1,247,267	-134,000	-0.11
339 Federated Department Stores	0	2,323,546	-352,000	-0.15
348 Mercantile Stores Co	0	626,305	-100,000	-0.16
379 Waban Inc.	0	423,026	-89,000	-0.21
405 Woolworth Corp.	0	2,615,000	-705,000	-0.27
409 K Mart Corp.	0	7,636,000	-2,119,000	-0.28

Industry: Drug Distribution

159 Eckerd Corp.	0	857,980	24,000	0.03
173 Rite Aid Corp.	0	847,747	21,000	0.02
174 McKesson Corp.	0	886,800	17,000	0.02
203 Walgreen Co.	0	1,929,630	-4,000	0.00
237 Longs Drug Stores Inc.	0	553,881	-12,000	-0.02
294 Bergen Brunswig Corp.	0	330,825	-27,000	-0.08
343 Cardinal Health Inc.	0	67,760	-11,000	-0.16
400 National Intergroup, Inc.	0	292,647	-77,000	-0.26

Industry: Drugs & Research

10 Amgen Inc.	255,321	328,427	427,000	0.73
20 Merck & Co., Inc.	1,172,800	2,913,900	1,625,000	0.40
25 IVAX Corp.	24,109	149,034	60,000	0.35
30 American Home Products	662,689	2,922,579	1,095,000	0.31
35 Schering-Plough Corp.	577,600	1,747,400	628,000	0.27
43 Bristol-Myers Squibb Co.	1,128,000	4,353,000	1,219,000	0.22
59 Sigma Aldrich Corp.	0	237,179	37,000	0.16
74 Rhone-Poulenc Rorer, Inc.	561,200	1,467,800	270,000	0.13
123 Lilly [Eli] and Co.	954,600	1,713,500	151,000	0.06
187 Upjohn Co.	642,033	1,409,149	25,000	0.01
188 Allergan, Inc.	102,500	362,200	3,000	0.01

223 Warner-Lambert Co.	464,900	2,596,100	-27,000	-0.01
249 Pfizer Inc.	974,400	3,066,000	-108,000	-0.03
305 Carter-Wallace, Inc.	49,903	325,742	-32,000	-0.09
456 American Cyanamid Co.	595,600	1,607,300	-1,077,000	-0.49

Industry: Eating Places

66 McDonald's Corp.	0	2,079,400	284,000	0.14
201 Marriott International, Inc.	0	5,739,000	-19,000	0.00
436 Flagstar Companies Inc.	0	2,127,453	-782,000	-0.37
547 Host Marriott Corp.	0	63,000	-437,000	-6.94

Industry: Electrical Products

68 Emerson Electric Co.	0	1,606,600	226,000	0.14
131 MagneTek, Inc.	0	229,007	14,000	0.06
190 Thomas & Betts Corp.	22,564	225,883	2,000	0.01
191 Hubbell Inc.	0	192,690	2,000	0.01
209 National Service Industries	0	557,011	1,000	0.00
386 Reliance Electric Co.	0	272,000	-59,000	-0.22
408 Raychem Corp.	128,992	479,889	-172,000	-0.28
428 Ametek, Inc.	0	76,759	-26,000	-0.34
433 Cooper Industries, Inc.	0	1,012,900	-369,000	-0.36
472 Westinghouse Electric Corp.	0	1,591,000	-941,000	-0.59

Industry: Electronics

29 Raytheon Co.	279,448	827,551	353,000	0.32
86 Motorola, Inc.	0	3,776,000	368,000	0.10
98 E-Systems, Inc.	0	161,870	15,000	0.09
162 General Instrument Corp.	73,741	149,362	6,000	0.03
178 Loral Corp.	0	3,039,149	48,000	0.02
208 Vishay Intertechnology	0	125,565	100	0.00
228 SCI Systems, Inc.	0	1,641,283	-15,000	-0.01
330 Varian Associates, Inc.	73,932	282,208	-48,000	-0.13
356 Harris Corp.	0	823,000	-138,000	-0.17
452 Litton Industries, Inc.	0	354,826	-164,000	-0.46

Industry: Entertainment

371 Paramount Communications	0	621,400	-118,000	-0.19
524 Disney [Walt] Co.	0	164,200	-215,000	-1.31

Industry: Food Distribution

138 Sysco Corp.	0	1,427,394	68,000	0.05
189 International Multifoods	0	197,515	2,000	0.01
354 Fleming Companies, Inc.	0	558,470	-94,000	-0.17

Industry: Food Processing

48 Wrigley [Wm.] Jr. Co.	0	542,944	98,000	0.18
52 Kellogg Co.	0	2,237,500	376,000	0.17
67 Heinz [H.J.] Co.	0	1,711,926	241,000	0.14
79 Gerber Products Co.	0	376,625	47,000	0.12
80 General Mills, Inc.	0	2,645,200	305,000	0.12
83 Lancaster Colony Corp.	0	125,079	14,000	0.11
97 CPC International Inc.	49,300	1,775,800	158,000	0.09
104 IBP, Inc.	0	96,626	8,000	0.08
115 Quaker Oats Co.	0	2,279,400	150,000	0.07
127 McCormick & Co. Inc.	0	422,700	27,000	0.06
128 Hershey Foods Corp.	0	1,035,519	62,000	0.06
129 Dean Foods Co.	0	391,061	24,000	0.06
148 Ralston Purina Group	0	2,755,300	97,000	0.04
149 Interstate Bakeries Corp.	0	472,602	18,000	0.04
161 Tyson Foods, Inc.	0	504,562	17,000	0.03
176 Hormel [Geo. A.] & Co.	0	491,734	11,000	0.02
177 Flowers Industries, Inc.	0	380,975	7,000	0.02
205 Sara Lee Corp.	0	4,377,000	17,000	0.00
206 ConAgra, Inc.	0	2,014,300	-7,000	0.00
207 Campbell Soup Co.	68,800	1,515,000	4,000	0.00
334 Archer-Daniels-Midland Co.	0	324,793	-46,000	-0.14
422 Pet Inc.	0	527,600	-163,000	-0.31
437 Savannah Foods & Inds.	0	57,102	-21,000	-0.37
439 Dole Food Co., Inc.	0	365,250	-137,000	-0.38
462 Chiquita Brands Intl.	0	332,934	-172,000	-0.52
470 Borden, Inc.	0	1,338,600	-765,000	-0.57

Industry: Food Retailing

124 Winn-Dixie Stores, Inc.	0	2,196,721	123,000	0.06
125 Stop & Shop Companies	0	685,847	41,000	0.06
126 Albertson's Inc.	0	2,161,561	127,000	0.06
137 Kroger Co.	0	4,314,777	212,000	0.05
160 Penn Traffic Co.	0	559,729	16,000	0.03
224 Vons Companies [The], Inc.	0	1,065,400	-7,000	-0.01
225 Giant Food Inc.	0	869,032	-13,000	-0.01
226 Bruno's, Inc.	0	489,950	-7,000	-0.01
250 Safeway Inc.	0	3,689,600	-96,000	-0.03
251 American Stores Co.	0	4,305,950	-145,000	-0.03
266 Southland Corp.	0	1,550,450	-78,000	-0.05
297 Smiths Food & Drug Centers	0	430,258	-36,000	-0.08
298 Great Atlantic & Pacific Tea	0	2,943,249	-242,000	-0.08
345 Food Lion Inc.	0	1,096,306	-179,000	-0.16

Industry: Forest Products

7 Louisiana-Pacific Corp.	0	115,600	92,000	0.80
378 Willamette Industries, Inc.	0	174,413	-37,000	-0.21
467 Georgia-Pacific Corp.	0	1,190,000	-642,000	-0.54
523 Boise Cascade Corp.	0	321,650	-385,000	-1.20

Industry: General Manufacturing

50 First Brands Corp.	0	257,799	43,000	0.17
57 Hillenbrand Industries, Inc.	0	466,116	74,000	0.16
72 Newell Co.	0	257,186	34,000	0.13
78 Illinois Tool Works Inc.	0	629,459	76,000	0.12
92 Rubbermaid Inc.	0	328,741	28,000	0.09
114 Minnesota Mining & Mfg.	0	3,535,000	263,000	0.07
156 Harsco Corp.	5,167	182,794	6,000	0.03
199 Crane Co.	0	178,381	100	0.00
221 Mark IV Industries, Inc.	28,620	240,192	-3,000	-0.01
248 Duracell International Inc.	0	795,200	-21,000	-0.03
291 Jostens, Inc.	0	353,881	-27,000	-0.08
321 Avery Dennison Corp.	0	642,700	-80,000	-0.12
329 Corning Inc.	173,100	774,000	-127,000	-013

399 Parker-Hannifin Corp.	0	333,644	-88,000	0.26
449 TRINOVA Corp.	55,314	246,221	-131,000	-0.43

Industry: Health Care Services

44 United Healthcare Corp.	0	408,534	87,000	0.21
51 Caremark International Inc.	0	241,400	40,000	0.17
58 Foundation Health Corp.	0	260,816	43,000	0.16
136 Humana Inc.	0	368,000	20,000	0.05
158 FHP International Corp.	0	269,645	9,000	0.03
263 Healthtrust Inc.	0	384,871	-18,000	-0.05
283 Beverly Enterprises, Inc.	0	1,062,162	-72,000	-0.07
293 National Medical Enterprises	0	3,163,000	-247,000	-0.08
421 American Medical Holdings	0	653,749	-204,000	-0.31

Industry: Industr. Distrib Services

39 Arrow Electronics, Inc.	0	314,323	77,000	0.24
55 Genuine Parts Co.	0	935,427	148,000	0.16
169 Grainger [W.W.] Inc.	0	722,704	11,000	0.02
217 Avnet, Inc.	0	383,997	-3,000	-0.01

Industry: Instruments

130 Honeywell Inc.	337,400	1,075,700	82,000	0.06
227 Perkin-Elmer Corp.	83,847	304,852	-3,000	-0.01
238 Thermo Electron Corp.	0	283,590	-5,000	-0.02
346 Johnson Controls Inc.	0	635,100	-101,000	-0.16
347 Beckman Instruments, Inc.	93,300	278,500	-59,000	-0.16
427 Tektronix, Inc.	157,068	395,698	-180,000	-0.33
532 Imo Industries Inc.	11,332	135,002	-277,000	-1.89

Industry: Machine & Hand Tools

155 Danaher Corp.	0	180,236	6,000	0.03
220 Snap-On Tools Corp.	27,700	482,210	-5,000	-0.01
290 Stanley Works [The]	0	512,300	-39,000	-0.08
389 Black & Decker Corp.	0	1,320,700	-300,000	-0.23
432 Cincinnati Milacron Inc.	0	191,300	-68,000	-0.36

451 SPX Corp.	0	215,131	-100,000	-0.46

Industry: Medical Products

23 Abbott Laboratories	880,974	1,918,176	1,036,000	0.37
24 Kendall International, Inc.	0	199,110	69,000	0.35
94 Medtronic, Inc.	132,955	480,006	54,000	0.09
95 Johnson & Johnson	1,182,000	5,771,000	654,000	0.09
172 Bausch & Lomb Inc.	57,864	672,022	11,000	0.02
259 Becton, Dickinson & Co.	139,141	660,508	-29,000	-0.04
372 Baxter International, Inc.	337,000	1,879,000	-435,000	-0.20
417 US Surgical Corp.	50,800	449,300	-144,000	-0.29

Industry: Other Leisure

65 Mattel Inc.	0	934,803	133,000	0.14
157 Hasbro, Inc.	280,571	897,484	32,000	0.03
186 Fleetwood Enterprises, Inc.	0	302,190	3,000	0.01
200 Polaroid Corp.	0	807,000	3,000	0.00
274 American Greetings Corp.	0	818,967	-52,000	-0.06
292 Harley-Davidson, Inc.	0	210,329	-16,000	-0.08
361 Eastman Kodak Co.	1,301,000	4,989,000	-1,114,000	-0.18
418 Brunswick Corp.	0	470,400	-143,000	-0.30
443 Tyco Toys, Inc.	0	315,762	-122,000	-0.39
499 Outboard Marine Corp.	0	226,100	-190,000	-0.84

Industry: Other Metals

42 Newmont Mining Corp.	52,694	50,286	23,000	0.22
392 Homestake Mining Co.	17,457	45,045	-15,000	-0.24
508 Cyprus Amax Minerals Co.	24,692	69,873	-95,000	-1.00
515 Phelps Dodge Corp.	56,775	103,744	-170,000	-1.06
517 Freeport-McMoRan Inc.	65,080	169,059	-255,000	-1.09
535 Magma Copper Co.	9,352	22,080	-72,000	-2.29
538 Asarco Inc.	20,871	107,646	-326,000	-2.54

Industry: Other Services

144 Olsten Corp.	0	561,956	25,000	0.04
145 Kelly Services, Inc.	0	316,838	12,000	0.04

257 First Financial Management	0	1,307,709	-49,000	--0.04
328 Manpower, Inc.	0	542,319	-69,000	-0.13
412 PHH Corp.	0	284,238	-82,000	-0.29
497 Borg-Warner Security Corp.	0	197,000	-164,000	-0.83
511 Safety-Kleen Corp.	0	19,037	-123,000	-1.03

Industry: Paper

90 Kimberly-Clark Corp.	158,500	1,439,500	142,000	0.09
398 Weyerhaeuser Co.	44,456	944,848	-254,000	-0.26
413 Mead [The] Corp.	0	685,100	-197,000	-0.29
458 Chesapeake Corp.	0	102,100	-51,000	-0.50
461 International Paper Co.	0	1,786,000	-926,000	-0.52
471 Scott Paper Co.	232,200	598,700	-481,000	-0.58
481 Consolidated Papers, Inc.	0	62,097	-42,000	-0.68
489 James River Corp. Of Va.	0	677,586	-518,000	-0.76
498 Union Camp Corp.	0	305,616	-255,000	-0.83
501 Westvaco Corp.	0	207,102	-184,000	-0.89
519 Potlatch Corp.	0	83,958	-95,000	-1.13
520 Manville Corp.	37,358	259,632	-337,000	-1.13
537 Champion International Corp.	0	292,684	-725,000	-2.48
544 Bowater Inc.	0	71,805	-351,000	-4.89

Industry: Paper Containers

61 Sonoco Products Co.	0	209,309	34,000	0.16
316 Temple-Inland Inc.	0	2,573,461	-291,000	-0.11
375 Bemis Co., Inc.	14,084	161,598	-36,000	-0.20
455 Longview Fibre Co.	0	49,994	-24,000	-0.48
465 ACX Technologies, Inc.	14,352	65,612	-42,000	-0.53
526 Stone Container Corp.	0	512,200	-781,000	-1.52
541 Federal Paper Board Co.	0	60,149	-163,000	-2.71

Industry: Personal Care

100 Colgate-Palmolive Co.	0	2,457,100	211,000	0.09
101 Clorox Co.	42,445	570,616	53,000	0.09
117 Gillette Co.	0	2,279,200	150,000	0.07
118 Block Drug Co., Inc.	0	367,150	27,000	0.07
133 Avon Products, Inc.	0	2,008,000	116,000	0.06

140 Stanhome Inc.	0	363,452	19,000	0.05
211 Alberto-Culver Co.	0	511,274	2,000	0.00
230 Ecolab Inc.	0	466,645	-4,000	-0.01
254 NCH Corp.	0	277,034	-7,000	-0.03
286 Procter & Gamble Co.	0	9,589,000	-658,000	-0.07

Industry: Petroleum Services

204 Dresser Industries, Inc.	0	887,500	-2,000	0.00
363 Baker Hughes Inc.	102,057	811,659	-169,000	-0.18
450 CBI Industries, Inc.	0	235,861	-107,000	-0.45
529 Halliburton Co.	0	218,400	-354,000	-1.62

Industry: Pollution Control

241 WMX Technologies, Inc.	0	1,678,202	-57,000	-0.03
368 Browning-Ferris Industries	0	559,419	-109,000	-0.19

Industry: Printing & Advertising

1 Valassis Communications Inc.	0	48,334	100,000	2.07
54 Omnicom Group Inc.	0	467,468	73,000	0.16
102 Banta Corp.	0	87,812	7,000	0.08
112 Interpublic Group of Cos.	0	618,466	45,000	0.07
360 Donnelley [R.R.] & Sons Co.	0	453,986	-83,000	-0.18

Industry: Publishing

71 Gannett Co, Inc.	0	650,390	87,000	0.13
82 Washington Post Co.	0	393,196	44,000	0.11
184 Reader's Digest Association	0	1,404,787	20,000	0.01
185 Dun & Bradstreet Corp.	0	3,506,700	27,000	0.01
218 Times Mirror [The] Co.	0	1,379,595	-15,000	-0.01
235 Dow Jones & Co., Inc.	0	598,292	-9,000	-0.02
242 Tribune Co.	0	495,000	-14,000	-0.03
243 McGraw-Hill, Inc.	0	774,160	-26,000	-0.03
244 Knight-Ridder, Inc.	0	665,509	-19,000	-0.03
304 Meredith Corp.	0	375,045	-32,000	-0.09
383 New York Times [The] Co.	0	756,460	-163,000	-0.22
440 Western Publishing Group	0	188,161	-74,000	-0.39

500 Time Warner Inc.	0	2,283,000	-1,998,000	-0.88

Industry: Railroads

31 Illinois Central Corp.	0	34,300	10,000	0.29
111 Kansas City Southern Inds.	0	749,000	54,000	0.07
233 Chicago & North Western	0	829,100	-18,000	-0.02
256 Burlington Northern Inc.	0	1,315,000	-48,000	-0.04
302 Union Pacific Corp.	0	1,679,000	-158,000	-0.09
303 CSX Corp.	0	7,934,000	-693,000	-0.09
310 Santa Fe Pacific Corp.	0	2,303,600	-235,000	-0.10
366 Southern Pacific Rail Corp.	0	1,079,700	-210,000	-0.19
390 Norfolk Southern Corp.	0	1,668,000	-396,000	-0.24

Industry: Semiconductors

9 Intel Corp.	970,000	1,168,000	1,609,000	0.75
40 Solectron Corp.	3,763	41,965	11,000	0.24
84 Advanced Micro Devices	262,802	290,861	61,000	0.11
105 Micron Technology Inc.	57,323	87,863	12,000	0.08
252 Texas Instruments Inc.	0	1,521,000	-43,000	-0.03
275 AMP Inc.	0	616,568	-39,000	-0.06
324 Molex Inc.	0	219,704	-27,000	-0.12
335 National Semiconductor Corp.	202,300	284,800	284,800	-0.14
355 Analog Devices, Inc.	94,107	158,675	-43,000	-0.17
374 LSI Logic Corp.	78,995	117,452	-40,000	-0.20

Industry: Special Machinery

13 Stewart & Stevenson Services	0	61,168	31,000	0.51
33 Briggs & Stratton Corp.	0	83,176	24,000	0.29
135 Pentair Inc.	0	223,596	12,000	0.05
197 Dover Corp.	0	496,789	1,000	0.00
198 Applied Materials Inc.	140,161	171,654	-1,000	0.00
247 Varity Corp.	80,100	358,100	-15,000	-0.03
281 FMC Corp.	149,244	539,432	-50,000	-0.07
320 Tyco International Inc.	0	506,729	-59,000	-0.12
342 General Signal Corp.	0	308,370	-50,000	-0.16
352 Interlake [The] Corp.	0	117,025	-20,000	-0.17
420 Caterpillar Inc.	319,000	1,423,000	-536,000	-0.31

430 Ingersoll-Rand Co.	0	707,867	-251,000	-0.35
446 Clark Equipment Co.	0	118,504	-49,000	-0.41
460 Deere & Co.	269,800	845,000	-552,000	-0.50
469 Harnischfeger Industries	0	211,183	-121,000	-0.57
474 NACCO Industries, Inc.	0	211,936	-131,000	-0.62
492 Timken [The] Co.	0	274,141	-214,000	-0.78

Industry: Steel

19 Nucor Corp.	0	87,583	35,000	0.40
26 Worthington Industries	0	68,809	23,000	0.33
393 Oregon Steel Mills, Inc.	0	46,727	-11,000	-0.24
453 Lukens Inc.	0	59,945	-29,000	-0.48
454 Allegheny Ludlum Corp.	41,901	46,048	-42,000	-0.48
527 Inland Steel Industries	-6,000	250,300	-383,000	-1.57
539 Wheeling-Pittsburgh Steel	0	63,383	-162,000	-2.56
542 National Steel Corp.	0	136,656	-379,000	-2.77
543 Armco Inc.	0	125,000	-497,000	-3.98
546 Bethlehem Steel Corp.	0	156,900	-980,000	-6.25
548 LTV Corp.	0	90,000	-1,556,000	-17.29

Industry: Telephone Companies

53 Alltel Corp.	0	1,066,326	174,000	0.16
279 Bell Atlantic Corp.	0	7,802,900	-519,000	-0.07
287 GTE Corp.	0	15,343,000	-1,192,000	-0.08
337 Southwestern Bell Corp.	0	2,916,100	-439,000	-0.15
382 Pacific Telesis Group	0	5,415,000	-1,192,000	-0.22
388 NYNEX Corp.	0	6,511,100	-1,499,000	-0.23
397 US West, Inc.	0	4,047,700	-1,039,000	-0.26
478 BellSouth Corp.	0	3,487,900	-2,337,000	-0.67

Industry: Telephone Equipment & Services

37 DSC Communications Corp.	86,620	121,173	52,000	0.25
121 MCI Communications Corp.	0	3,310,000	187,000	0.06
152 Sprint Corp.	0	8,466,000	235,000	0.03
234 AT&T	3,069,000	17,280,000	-466,000	-0.02
394 Scientific-Atlanta, Inc.	60,161	114,040	-43,000	-0.25
549 McCaw Cellular Comm.	0	22,343	-616,000	-27.57

Industry: Textiles

2 Unifi Inc.	0	35,713	63,000	1.76
27 Cone Mills Corp.	0	73,326	24,000	0.33
91 Shaw Industries, Inc.	0	280,529	24,000	0.09
341 Interface Inc.	0	151,576	-24,000	-0.16
370 Burlington Industries Equity	0	147,270	-28,000	-0.19
407 Springs Industries, Inc.	0	281,539	-79,000	-0.28
415 Westpoint Stevens Inc.	0	192,138	-55,000	-0.29
416 Fieldcrest Cannon, Inc.	0	101,843	-30,000	-0.29
442 TRIARC Companies Inc.	0	214,020	-84,000	-0.39

Industry: Tire & Rubber

47 Cooper Tire & Rubber Co.	0	62,282	12,000	0.19
307 Goodyear Tire & Rubber	0	1,922,100	-174,000	-0.09

Industry: Tobacco

8 UST Inc.	0	299,206	232,000	0.78
62 Universal Corp.	0	247,325	39,000	0.16
99 Dibrell Brothers, Inc.	0	81,875	7,000	0.09
116 Philip Morris Companies Inc.	0	25,974,000	1,887,000	0.07
180 American Brands, Inc.	0	7,917,300	180,000	0.02
306 Standard Commercial Corp.	0	74,406	-7,000	-0.09
438 RJR Nabisco Holdings Corp.	0	5,731,000	-2,134,000	-0.37

Industry: Transport Services

278 Federal Express Corp.	0	2,155,958	-150,000	-0.07
309 Ryder System, Inc.	0	3,339,127	-344,000	-0.10
359 Airborne Freight Corp.	0	190,546	-35,000	-0.18
377 Trinity Industries, Inc.	0	93,400	-20,000	-0.21
521 GATX Corp.	0	152,400	-176,000	-1.15

Industry: Trucking & Shipping

143 Greyhound Lines Inc.	0	323,846	12,000	0.04
196 Hunt [JB] Transport Services	0	70,128	100	0.00

216 Roadway Services, Inc.	0	95,136	-1,000	-0.01
314 TNT Freightways Corp.	0	44,827	-5,000	-0.11
351 Alexander & Baldwin, Inc.	0	104,337	-18,000	-0.17
423 Consolidated Freightways	0	528,022	-171,000	-0.32
466 Yellow Freight System, Inc.	0	126,849	-68,000	-0.54
510 American President Cos.	0	64,281	-66,000	-1.03

APPENDIX B

Glossary, Acronyms, and Abbreviations

Address (network address)—Internet site addresses come in two forms: (1) as a set of thirty-two bit numbers, commonly expressed as a sequence of four decimal numbers such as 192.168.0.1, and (2) as alphanumerics such as mail.tpp.com. These can represent the same address, and either could be used, for example, with Telnet. People find the alphanumerics easier to remember than numbers. My own E-mail address at this site would be noted as amaitra@mail.tpp.com.

Anchor—A marker for the beginning or the end of a hypertext link.

Anonymous FTP—Accessing data via the File Transfer Protocol, or FTP, using the special user name "anonymous." This method provides restricted access to public data.

Archie—A service used to search thousands of FTP sites for any directory name, filename, string of characters, or words that users specify.

ARPANET (Advanced Research Projects Agency Network)—The granddaddy of the Internet. It was the original communications network created by the Advanced Research Projects Agency, a branch of the United States Department of Defense. It was designed to withstand any unforeseen events and give America the edge in any conflict.

ASCII (American Standard Code for Information Interchange)—A worldwide standard in which the numbers, uppercase letters, lowercase letters, some punctuation marks, some symbols, and some control codes have been assigned numbers from zero to 127. For instance, when using ASCII, the letter "a" is always stored as binary number 1000001. Documents created using only the ASCII characters are very easy to transfer over the Internet.

Authoring Tool—A program which partially automates the process of writing HTML.

Backbone—Refers to a high-speed network that links mid-level networks. It is used to expedite data passage from source to destination, where data is stored on computers or servers in various locations around the globe.

BBS (Bulletin Board System)—This is a remote computer user interface offering a way to post public messages in various topical discussion groups, receive files from and send files to the public, and access other remote computers and services via the Internet and/or through direct dial-up.

Binary—Refers to any data stored or transferred in digital form.

BITNET—An acronym for "Because It's Time Network." It is a global academic and research network started in 1981 and operated by EDUCOM.

Body—Refers to the main text or content of an HTML document.

Bounce—If an E-mail is undelivered, it is sent back (bounced) to the sender so that she or he will know the mail was not delivered.

Browser—A Web client program (eg. Mosaic, Netscape.) which sends requests for resources across networks and displays those resources when they are received.

Button—A graphical representation of a button on an area of a screen that is designed to be "clicked on" or otherwise selected for user input.

Campuswide Information System (CWIS)—A tool used for navigation and information retrieval. It provides data from a variety of campus sources available through one user interface.

CERN—The European Laboratory for Particle Physics in Geneva, Switzerland, where the Web was first developed. The acronym CERN comes from the earlier French title: "Conseil Europeen pour la Recherche Nucleaire."

Client/Server—Refers to information distribution on a network using a small number of server programs to provide data to client programs installed on many computers through-out the network. The database is maintained by the server program and, if and when requested by client programs, the server program retrieves information from the database and sends the information through the network to the client programs. The client programs offer a user-friendly and consistent interface.

Communications Software—Refers to programs running on a personal computer that allow the computer to communicate with a modem, and thus through the phone lines.

Cracker—A person using computer knowledge to attempt access to computer systems with the intention of maliciously damaging those systems and/or data in them.

Dial-in (also Dial-up)—Connection between two computers over standard voice grade telephone lines, usually via modems.

Discussion List—This is similar in some ways to mailing list. The major difference is that the mailing list is sent to subscribers in one batch, whereas a discussion list forwards messages one at a time.

Domain Name—A group of names listed with dots (.) between them. This is an Internet addressing system. Inter-Networking Information Center (InterNIC) of Network Solutions, Inc. assigns and keeps track of all domain names in the United States where the most general domains are network categories such as edu (education), com (commercial), and gov (government). Countries use two-letter abbreviations such as ca (Canada), au (Australia), ch (Switzerland), de (Germany), it (Italy), nz (New Zealand), and sg (Singapore).

Download—To copy data from a remote computer to a local computer. The opposite is upload.

E-mail—A system used by computer users to exchange messages with other computer users (or group of users) via a communications network. E-mail is the basis for discussion groups and many other Internet/Intranet services.

E-zine—Refers to electronic magazines. These are the ultimate in do-it-yourself publishing.

Finger—An Internet system that allows the user to find out the name of a person who has an E-mail address, when the person last checked for mail, and several other items.

Freeware—Totally free software made available from many locations on the Internet (often via FTP).

FTP (File Transfer Protocol)—A protocol allowing a user on one host to access and transfer files to and from another host over the Internet.

FAQs (Frequently Asked Questions)—Newcomers arrive at Usenet newsgroups or E-mail lists all the time and want to find out the facts and guidelines about a particular topic and group. To respond to these newcomers, a document in question and answer format is assembled. These FAQs are revised at regular intervals to offer the most up-to-date information on a given subject.

Gateway—A computer that connects two or more networks, often to pass data between incompatible network systems.

GIF (Graphics Interchange Format)—CompuServe developed a type of picture storage file, now widely used on the Internet. Files in this format are designated by an extension of .gif.

Gopher—A widely used, menu-based storage system for files and links to other Internet resources. See chapter 2.

Host—Internet access provider's computer.

HTML—HyperText Markup Language used for World Wide Web documents.

HTTP—HyperText Transfer Protocol. This is the Internet protocol that allows Web clients to retrieve information from Web servers.

HyperText—Links information in a document to related information by address codes operating behind the scenes. A user simply clicks on highlighted text to call up more details on a topic or jump to a related topic—within one document or between documents. "Between documents" could mean anywhere on the World Wide Web (WWW).

Hytelnet—Frequently updated database, providing information about specific Telnet sites and aiding in connection to them.

Internet—A digital communications network connecting various other (smaller) networks from around the world. Started in the United States, it transfers data using a standardized protocol called TCP/IP.

Intranet—Refers to the use of the Internet technologies within the enterprise to enhance user productivity.

IRC (Internet Relay Chat)—A popular method used on the Internet in order to find quick answers in real time to questions on a variety of topics. This method does not have as far a reach as posting to a newsgroup.

Listserv—An automated program that accepts mail messages from users and does basic operations on mailing lists (discussion groups) for those users. Listserv answers requests for indexes, FAQs, archives of the previous discussions, and other files.

Login—Used interchangeably with "logon." Refers to a process where a user wants to establish a connection to another computer. The process involves some user steps, such as entering a specific login password.

Logoff—To leave or disconnect from a computer system. Often accomplished by selecting a menu item for disconnecting.

Mailing List—A list of E-mail addresses used to discuss a certain set of topics. Different mailing lists discuss different topics. In the Internet, for those mailing lists maintained by a human, rather than by a listserv, one can generally subscribe to a list by sending a mail message to: "listname-REQUEST@host" and entering a request to subscribe in the body of the message. To send messages to other subscribers, one needs to use the address "listname@host."

Majordomo—Refers to a mail server software.

Mosaic—A browser with a graphical user interface that enables users to forego standard text in place of graphics and sound. It is a public domain package, available free of charge from the National Center for Supercomputing Applications' (NCSA) Internet server.

MODEM (Modulator/DEModulator)—An electronic device that converts the digital signals used by computers into analog signals needed by voice telephone systems. Virtually all modems combine the send and receive functions in one circuit.

Moderator—The moderators in various discussion groups watch the postings to ensure that the language and nature of the messages are suitable for public postings and that those postings relate to the overall topics and goals of the list.

Netscape (TM)—Refers to Netscape Communications Corporation's client software for enterprise networks and the Internet.

Network—Computers connected to facilitate data transmission amongst them. See chapter 2.

Network Access Provider (Network Service Provider)—Any organization that provides network connectivity or dial-up access.

NIC (Network Information Center)—A central place that maintains information about a network within the Internet. Most network service providers also provide an NIC for their users.

Node—Refers to a computer that is directly connected to a network and is used to transfer and route data or provide end-user services.

NSFNET (National Science Foundation Network)—The system that the National Science Foundation, a United States federal agency, created for high-speed data transfer links and nodes. It initially formed the backbone of the Internet.

Online—Refers to activity being carried out while a computer is connected to another computer or network.

PPP (Point to Point Protocol)—Refers to TCP/IP connections that use serial lines such as dial-up telephone lines. Similar to SLIP (see below), but it is a later standard that offers features such as compression, better flow control, etc.

Protocol—Represents a formal description of message formats involving timing, error control, etc., and a set of operating rules of data transmissions and other activities on a network.

RFC (Requests For Comments)—The document series begun in 1969 that describes the Internet systems, protocols, proposals, etc.

Real Time—Describes particular moments when two or more people are communicating via computers at the same instant.

Shareware—Software, initially available free, with authors expecting voluntary payments after an initial test period. There are functional limitations in the initial versions, with the promise of an upgrade available if the fee is paid. Usually reasonable prices.

SLIP (Serial Line Internet Protocol)—Refers to TCP/IP connections that use serial lines such as dial-up telephone lines. This is generally used at sites with few users as a cheaper alternative than a full Internet connection. SLIP is being replaced by PPP at many sites.

TCP/IP (Transmission Control Protocol/Internet Protocol)—Represents two major communications protocols used within the Internet: TCP and IP. These, along with several others, form the foundation for communications between hosts in the Internet. The various service protocols, such as FTP, Telnet, etc., use TCP/IP to transfer information.

Telnet—This Internet standard protocol is for remote terminal connection service.

Upload—Refers to copying data from a local computer to a remote computer. The opposite is download.

URL (Uniform Resource Locator)—Refers to the addressing scheme for resources on the Web.

USENET Newsgroups—Like Listservs and mailing lists, these serve as forums for discussion on any given topic of interest. Messages posted to USENET usually are echoed to servers across the globe, allowing businesses to keep current with related corporate news and products, while broadening their exposure to thousands and even millions of Internet users.

User Name—Either assigned by an Internet Service Provider (ISP) or selected by an individual user, this represents a short name unique to a user on his or her ISP's system. This name, followed by an individual's site address, becomes the user's E-mail address.

UUCP (Unix to Unix Copy Program)—This was initially a protocol for communicating between consenting Unix systems via dial-up phone lines. The term is more commonly used today to describe a large international network which uses the UUCP protocol to pass news and electronic mail.

Veronica—Refers to a method used for searching available Gopher sites for information on a specific topic.

Virtual Reality—Refers to combinations of user-interface involving three-dimensional graphics, speech synthesis, speech recognition, and other features that closely mimic humans' normal operating experiences in the real world.

WAIS (Wide Area Information Service)—Refers to an indexing mechanism for larger databases.

WWW (World Wide Web or the Web)—Refers to the hypertext-based, distributed information system created by researchers at CERN in Switzerland. The WWW servers are interconnected to allow a user to traverse the Web from any starting point.

APPENDIX C

Hardware and Software Issues

The author hopes that after reading this book, many of you will conclude that the Internet's extraordinary array of inexpensive global communication resources makes it an indispensable part of a contemporary enterprise. At this time many enterprises still have little or no experience with the Internet's technologies. Effective enterprise integration with the Internet requires a solid understanding of hardware and software solutions relative to connecting to the Net, setting up an Internet server, assigning hostnames and IP numbers, providing TCP/IP services, and choosing a package of client software. This appendix is for those who are not at all conversant with the TCP/IP, Unix, or the Internet. For those people, the best approach to Internet connectivity is to: (a) review and stock up on books that describe the various Internet connectivity options and (b) initially contract with an outside provider who can offer a total Internet solution.

For individual accounts, the service providers offer shell accounts. These enable individuals to access the Internet by logging in to a remote Unix host using a simple dial-up terminal program, and then running Internet client software on the remote machine. The shell user's local computer is not directly connected to the Internet, but acts as a "dumb" terminal.

Many service providers will, for an additional fee, register a domain name for shell or SLIP/PPP users and configure their systems to permit mail to be sent to that address. However, this does not remove all the limitations. The following books are recommended for understanding the hardware and software issues connected with the various configuration options:

Kehoe, Brendan, *Zen and the Art of the Internet: A Beginner's Guide*, Englewood Cliffs, NJ: Prentice Hall, 1992.

Krol, E., *The Whole Internet User's Guide & Catalog*, Sebastopol, CA: O'Reilly & Associates, Inc., 1992.

LaQuey, T., *The Internet Companion: A Beginner's Guide to Global Networking*, Reading, MA: Addison-Wesley Publishing Company, 1992.

Levine, John and Carol Baroudi, *Internet Secrets,* IDG Books Worldwide, 1995.

Marine, A., S. Kirkpatrick, V. Neou, and C. Ward, *Internet: Getting Started*, Englewood Cliffs, NJ: Prentice Hall, 1993.

209

APPENDIX D

Professional and Business Resources on the Internet

This category is like a moving target because a printed list of Internet resources is out of date even before it goes to press. Accordingly, books that are long and claim to cover all the resource directories often will have old and even inaccurate source materials. They are definitely not recommended. Online resources offer the most up-to-date information on any topic of interest.

For instance, Internet Direct and I-Site are the sponsors of The List, the most comprehensive list of Internet service providers. They are listed by country, country code, and area code. The National Center of Supercomputer Applications in Illinois is featuring The List on their home page. There are only four centers in the United States. Yahoo used to have the world's second largest alphabetical list of service providers, but Yahoo now recommends The List as the preferred place to find a new provider. To review The List online, go to: http://thelist.com/

If you want discipline-specific resources, a simple query on Internet Resources Guide offers information on:

(1) Internet Legal Resources

This pertains to law and the legal profession and is meant for everybody, including lay persons and legal scholars. It covers such topics as law firms and lawyers on the Internet, law school directories, law student services, law references and resources, legal associations, organizations, and services, law-related newsgroups, United States Federal Judicial Decisions, and so on.

(2) Internet Advertising Resources

The resources of advertising on the Internet have been experiencing rapid growth. This guide provides links to select sources of information about advertising and marketing on the Internet, arranged by subjects such as "Print Publications on Advertising on the Internet, "Business Presence on the Internet," and "Acceptable Advertising Practices on the Internet."

(3) Corporate Resources

Of particular interest to an investor might be the story behind the symbol of a company or companies. The Hastings Group has designed Corporate Profiles at http://www.stock-profiles.com.corporate.html to provide information in an easily accessible and digestable format. This allows an invester to make an informed decision fast. The Hastings Group has designed

(4) Organizational Resources

These include several different types of online reference resources. The following is a sampling of the variety that you can find.

ERIC (The Educational Resources Information Center) provides access to an extensive body of education-related literature. A portion of ERIC is AskERIC, an Internet-based question-answering service for teachers, library media specialists, and administrators. Drawing on the extensive resources of the ERIC system, AskERIC provides answers to most questions about primary and secondary education, learning, teaching, information technology, or educational administration.

InterNIC is a group funded by the United States National Science Foundation. It provides information services to the United States research and education networking commmunity.

Internet Society is an international membership organization for individuals and organizations that support its goals of promoting the use of the Internet. It provides a forum for exploration of new Internet applications, and stimulates collaboration among organizations in their operational use of the global Internet.

Asia Pacific Network Information Center is a cooperative organization of national network information centers in the Asia Pacific region operating under the auspices of the Asia Pacific Coordinating Committee for Intercontinental Research Networks. Its task is to provide information and registration services to networking organizations throughout Asia and the Pacific Rim regions.

(5) Business, Marketing, and Finance Resources

These include Usenet Newsgroups, small business information, magazines, journals, and serials covering accounting and legal, aerospace and defense, agriculture, automotive, banking, chemicals, communications, computing and electronics, consumer electronics, energy and fuel, entertainment, environmental sciences, financial services, forest products, general, government, healthcare, insurance, media, mining, non-U.S., regional business, transportation, and so on.

(6) Resources for the Professionals

The Internet resources, listed by profession, are constantly being updated. As part of the updating procedures, the resources are frequently relocated to different Internet locations. Therefore,it will not be prudent to cite any particular internet address here. Just be aware that there are a number of subject-specific sites available from Clearinghouse for Subject-Oriented Internet Resource Guides. The guides cover: high technology, science and engineering; space, satellite, and astronomy; natural resources and environment; allied health; biotechnology; journalism and publishing; education; law; computers, statistics and mathematics; agriculture; geography and land use; social sciences; international, and miscellaneous.

References

Introduction

[1]   Internet Week. Http://www.phillips.com:3200/sample.html and also an interview article, *"Weaving IBM's Web Plans," Information Week*, May 29, 1995, pp. 36-38

Chapter 1

[1]   Ellsworth, Jill H. And Mathew V. Ellsworth, *The Internet Business Book,* John Wiley & Sons, Inc., 1994

[2]   *Internet Domain Names Now Cost $50 Each Annually,* XINHUA via Individual, New York, 14 September 1995.

[3]   *Understanding the Basics of the Net,* HP Internet Primer, 1995, http://www.dmo.hp.com/gsyinternet/primer/main.html

[4]   *Internet vs. Intranet: Market Opportunities and Trends,* Zona Research, Inc., December 1995.

[5]   *Putting the Web to Work Inside Your Business: A White Paper,* Netscape Communications Corporation, 1996, http://home.netscape.com/comprod/at_work/index.html

[6]   Richman, Dan, "Fueling a Desired Change," *Information Week,* September 18, 1995, pp. 106-109.

[7]   Peterson, A. Padgett, "Firewall Security on the Internet,"A Report by Faulkner Information Services, Pennsauken, NJ, 1996.

[8]   Sprout, A. And Ruth Coxeter, "The Internet Inside Your Company," *FORTUNE*, November 27, 1995.

[9]   Reichard, Kevin, "Leveraging E-mail," *PC Magazine*, May 16, 1995, pp 241-245.

[10]   "Internet Primer," HP Open Enterprise Computing, 1995,
         http://www.dmo.hp.com/gsyinternet/primer/main.html

[11]   Ellsworth, _____, *op. cit.*

[12]   "Do you know who is reading your E-mail," SecureWare Press Release, July 1995,
         http://www.sware.com/whatsnew/pressrelease/070195.html

[13]   Reichard, Kevin, "Letting Customers Dig Through Your Data," *PC Magazine,*
         May 16, 1995, p. 233.

[14]   Peterson, _____, *op. cit.*

[15]   bid.

[16]   Reichard, Kevin, "Will Your Business Be Safe," *PC Magazine,* May 16, 1995,
         p. 218.

[17]   Ives, Blake and Sirkka Jarvenpaa, "The Internet : Background on the World
         Wide Web,"
         http://ox.smu.edu/mis/cases/webcase/wwww.html # linkmosaic

[18]   Gonzalez, Sean, "Building A Web Presence," *PC Magazine,* May 16, 1995, p.205.

[19]   "The Age of Hypercompetition," UUNET, undated,
         http://www.uu.net/busguide.htm

[20]   Ives,_____, *op. cit.*

[21]   "Netscape Integrats WYSIWYG Document Creation into Netscape Navigator to
         Enable Users to Easily Create, Edit, and Navigate Live Online Documents," *PR
         NEWSWIRE,* Mountrainview, CA, September 18, 1995.

[22]   Netscape Builds Momentum with Shipment of Netscape Navigator 2.0,"
         Netscape Press Release, Mountainview, CA February 5, 1996.

[23]   "Introducing Netscape Navigator Gold 2.0," *Data Sheet,* 1996 Netscape
         Communications Corporation,
         http//:home.netscape.com/comprod/products/navigator/gold/index.html

[24]   Miller, Stuart, "Understanding The Internet," A Report by Faulkner Information Services, Pennsauken, NJ, 1996.

[25]   Ibid.

[26]   "How Is the Web Being Used," HP Internet Primer, http://www.dmo.hp.com/gsyinternet/primer/hpprimer7.html

[27]   "Merit Retires NSFNET Backbone Service," *MichNet News*, Vol. P, No. 2; also available at gopher://nic.merit.edu:7043/0/nsfnet/nsfnet.retired.

[28]   "The Internet Grows Up," *PR NEWSWIRE*, Arlington, VA, September 14, 1995

[29]   Rupley, Sebastian, "Internet Survey Surprises," *PC Magazine* via Individual, September 24 1995.

[30]   Peterson,_____, *op. cit.*

[31]   Reichard, Kevin, "Will Your Business Be Safe," *PC Magazine*, May 16, 1995, p. 218.

[32]   "Consultation Paper On The Regulation Of Online Information Services," July 7, 1995, http://www.usyd.edu.au/~pete/cpreply.html

[33]   "White Paper InternetMCI Security Department," undated, http://www.security.mci.net/sec-whit.html

[34]   Reichard,_____, *op. cit.*

Chapter 2

[1]   Rhinelander, Thomas, et al., "CIO Meets Internet," The Forrester Report, Volume 12, Number 7, May, 1995.

[2]   http://www.uu.net/busguide.html

[3]   Rhinelander, et al., _____, *op. cit., p.* 8.

[4]   Winer, Robert, "Information Infrastructures for Integratd Enterprises," *Institute for Defense Analysis*, Volume 1, 1991.

[5]   Davidow, William, *The Virtual Corporation,* Harper-Collins Publishers, 1992.

[6]   Carver, Gary and Howard Bloom, "Concurrent Engineering Technical Program Description; System Integration for Manufacturing," *National Institute of Standards and Technology*, November, 1993.

[7]   "Contractor Integrated Technical Information Service: Business Case—Feasibility Study," Northrop Corporation, 1992.

[8]   O'Neil and Bertrand, "Developing a Winning JIT Marketing Strategy," 1991 referenced by William Davidow, *The Virtual Corporation,* Harper-Collins Publishers, 1992, p. 9.

[9]   Teresko, John, "Tripping Down the Information Superhighway," *Industry Week,* August 2, 1993, pp. 33-40.

[10]   Evans S., Pestotnik S. L., Classen D. C., and Burke J. P., "Development of an Automated Antibiotic Consultant," *M.D. Computing*, October, 1993, pp. 17-22.

[11]   Evans R. S., Reed M.G., Burke J. P., Pestotnik S.L., Larsen R.A., Classen D.C., and Clayton P.D., "Computerized Approach to Monitor Prophylactic Antibiotics," *Proceedings of the Eleventh Symposium on Computer Applications in Medical Care*, IEEE Computer Society Press, 1987, pp. 241-245].

[12]   "Workgroup for Electronic Data Interchange Report," *1993 WEDI Report,* Executive Summary, p. iii.

[13]   "Department of Transportation Strategic plan," U.S. Department of Transportation, January 1994.

[14]   U.S. Secretary of Transportation Federico Penna, "The IVHS Future looks Bright and It's Almost Here," *The Washington Times Supplement: Technology and the New Transportation,* May 23, 1994.

[15]   "Airport Passenger Processing System, White Paper," *Unisys,* 1991]

[16]   "S-Cubed Division of Maxwell Laboratories," *Business Wire,* June 21, 1994.

[17]   "Tracking through the Web," http://www.phillips.com:3200/sample.html.

[18]   Hoffman, Thomas, "Business Units, IS Benefit From Sharing Ideas," *Computer World,* January 10, 1995, p. 24.

[19]   Leeburg, Lewis E. and Bill J. Mann, "Managing the Integration of Information Technologies," *Information Management,* Vol. 8, Auerbach Publishers, Warren, Gorham & Lamont, 1991, p.7.

[20]   Parker, M. N. and R. J. Benson, "Enterprisewide Information Management: State-of-the-Art Strategic Planning," *Journal of Information Systems Management,* vol. 6, No.

3, 1989 referenced in Philip N. James, "Strategic and Long-Range Information Systems Planning," *Information Management,* W-12, Auerbach Publications, 1992.

Chapter 3

[1]   Rhinelander, Thomas, et al., "CIO Meets Internet," *The Forrester Report,* Volume 12, Number Seven, May, 1995.

[2]   Rhinelander,_____, *op. cit.*

[3]   Rhinelander,_____, *op. cit.,* p. 8

[4]   Ibid.

[5]   Vis, D. "AMR Lands on the Internet with Expensive Airline Site," *TRAVEL WEEKLY,* Volume 54, Number 41, May 25, 1995.

[6]   Stahl, Stephenie, "Technology Hits the Road," *INFORMATIONWEEK,* September 18, 1995, p. 192.

[7]   Hayes, Mary, "Focused on the Customer," *INFORMATIONWEEK,* September 18, 1995, pp. 92-96

[8]   "Internet Technology Industry to Reach $13 Billion in Five Years; Will Create Another $10 Billion in Related Services Mass Media at Formative Stage, Hambrecht & Quist Conference Told," *PR Newswire via Individual,* October 2, 1995.

[9]   Dellecave Jr., Tom, "Charged with Change," *INFORMATION WEEK,* September 18, 1995, pp. 100-104.

Chapter 4

[1]   "Leading Trends in Information Services," Seventh Annual Survey of North American Chief Information Executives—1995, Deloitte & Touche LLP Management Consulting.

[2]   Lyons, Daniel, "Lack of Hard Numbers Fails To Deter Stampede To The Web," *INFOWORLD*, November 5, 1995.

[3]   _____, *op. cit.*

[4]   INSIDE Gartner Group This Week, "The Second Age of IT: Increasing The Return on Technology," Vol. XI, No 41, October 11, 1995

[5]   Lyons, *op. cit.*

[6]   Hammer, M. And Mangurian, G., *"The Changing Value of Communication Technology,"* Sloan School of Management Review, Winter, 1987, pp. 65-67, Referenced in "The Internet Sales and Marketing Directions," *INPUT,* 1995, p. 27.

[7]   Stewart, Thomas A., "What Information Costs," Information Technology Special Report, *FORTUNE,* July 10, 1995, p. 119.

[8]   Referenced in Kiely, Thomas, "Variable Costs," *CIO Magazine,* February 15, 1994.

[9]   Kiely, *op. cit.*

[10]   LaPlante, Alice, "It's Got What It Takes," *COMPUTERWORLD*, October 3, 1994, p. 87.

[11]   Strassmann, Paul, "The Internet: A Way of Outsourcing Infomercenaries?," http://www.strassmann.com/pubs/infomerc.html.

[12]   _____, "Managing Capital Investment in Computers," http://www.strass mann.com/pubs/capital.html.

[13]   LaPlante, *op. cit.,* p. 88.

[14]   _____, *op. cit.,* p. 88.

[15]   Barth, Daniel L., "A Better Understanding," *CIO Magazine,* October 1, 1993.

[16]   LaPlante, *op. cit.,* p. 88.

[17]   _____, *op. cit.,* p. 88.

[18]   _____, *op. cit.,* p. 91.

[19]   INSIDE, *op. cit.,* p. 4.

[20]   LaPlante, *op. cit.,* p. 91.

[21]   _____, *op. cit.,* p. 91.

[22]   LaPlante, Alice and Alter, Allan E., "It All Adds Up," *COMPUTERWORLD*, October 31, 1994, p. 77.

[23]   _____, *op. cit.,* p. 77.

[24]   Lyons, *op. cit.,*

[25]   Lyons, *op. cit.*

[26]   Rash Jr., Wayne, "Demand Grows for Commercial Accountability on the Internet," *CommmunicationsWeek*, November 6, 1995, p. 86, http://techweb.cmp.com./cw .

[27]   Strassmann, Paul A., "Introduction To ROM(TM) Analysis: Linking Management Productivity and Information Technology," http://strassmann.com/consulting/ROM-intro/Intro_to_Rom.html.

[28]   Referenced in Paul A. Strassmann, "1993 Information Productivity (TM) Rankings, Industrial Companies," http://www.strassmann.com/consulting/ip-rankings.html.

[29]   Baatz, Elizabeth, "The Meaning of Value Gets a Fresh Definition," *CIO Magazine*, http://www.strassman.com/pubs/eva-cio.html.

[30]   Strassmann, *op. cit.,* p. 8.

[31]   Baatz, E. B., "Altered Stats," *CIO Magazine,* October 15, 1994, p. 44.

[32]   Pastore, Richard, "The Road To Recovery," *CIO Magazine,* January 1993, pp. 68-70; also, refer to "Strategies To Control Distributed Computing's Exploding Costs," *The Gartner Group Report* at http://www.gartner.com/hcigdist.htm.

Chapter 5

[1]   "FOCUS: Internet Policies," *WORK FORCE STRATEGIES—A Supplement to BNA's Employee Relations Weekly*, Volume 13, Number 33, August 21, 1995.

[2]   "Developing an Enterprise Internet Policy," Research Notes, Gartner Group, February 1995.

[3]   "Many Report Financial Losses and Internet Break-ins Due to Lax Computer Security," *PR Newswire* via Individual, Nov. 21, 1995.

[4]   Okon, Walter, "WWW Structure for DISA's Web," *A White Paper, DISA,* September, 1995.

[5]   "U.S. Judge Rules Internet Services May be Liable for Postings," *Los Angeles Time,* November 29, 1995.

[6]   "Developing an Enterprise Internet Policy," Research Notes, Gartner Group, March 1995.

[7]   Gibbs, M., "An Acceptable Use Policy Can Derail Internet Distractions," *Network World,* September 26, 1995.

[8]   High, Cliff of Tenax Software Engineering in Olympia, Washington was qouted in "FOCUS: Internet Policies," *WORKFORCE STRATEGIES—A Supplement To BNA's Employee Relations Weekly,* Volume 13, Number 33, August 21, 1995.

[9]   Chiu, Yvonne,"E-Mail Gives Rise to the E-Wall—A Blizzard of Personal Chat \ Raises Worries About Office Productivity," *The Washington Post,* August 18, 1995.

[10]   Gordon, Mark L. And Christopher L. Gallinari, "Don't Carry Nothin' Someone

Else Has Sold: Ease On Down The Electronic Road," A review article by Gordon and Glickson P.C., Chicago, IL, 1995.

[11]   McKenzie, Diana J.P., "How To Minimize The Legal Costs of Doing Business On The Information Superhighway," A review article by Gordon and Glickson P.C., Chicago, IL, 1995.

[12]   Weiss, Barry D., "Implementing Sound Corporate Internet Policies: Legal and Management Issues," A review article by Gordon and Glickson P.C., Chicago, IL, 1995.

[13]   Strangelove, Michael, "The Walls Come Down," *Internet World,* May 1995, p. 42, referenced in Barry D. Weiss, op. cit., p. 17.

[14]   Grzesik, Bob, "Psychotic E-Mail Can Make You Look Loonier Than You Are," Opinions in *INFOWORLD*, Volume 17, Issue 48, November 27, 1995.

[15]   Chiu,_____, *op. cit.*

[16]   Weiss,_____, *op. cit.*

[17]   McKenzie, Diana J. P., "Commerce On the Internet: Surfing Through Cyberspace Without Getting Wet," A review article by Gordon and Glickson P.C., Chicago, IL, 1995.

[18]   Fites, M., Kratz, P. And A. Brebner, "Control and Security of Computer nformation Systems," Computer Science Press, 1989, referenced in *Site Security Handbook.* Site Security Policy Handbook Working Group RFC 1244, July 1991.

[19]   Ranum, Marcus J., "Internet Firewalls Frequently Asked Questions," http:// www. iwi. com/pubs/faq.html.

Chapter 6

No entry

Chapter 7

[1]   Remarks by Nicholas Negroponte, as quoted by Vint Cerf in his "Keynote Address at Internet@Telecom95," Geneva, Switzerland, October 7, 1995, http://www3.itu.ch/TELECOM/pressdocs/papers/cerf2.html

[2]   Petrillo, John C., Keynote Address at Internet@Telcom95, Geneva, Switzerland, October 8, 1995,
        http://www3.itu.ch/TELECOM/pressdocs/papers/petrillo.html

[3]   "Jets On The Net," Press Clippings, July 31, 1995,
        http://home.netscape.comprod/at_work/press.clippings/computer_world.html

[4]   Clark, Jim, Kenote Address at Internet@Telecom95, Geneva, Switzerland, October 7, 1995,
        http://www3.itu.ch/TELECOM/pressdocs/papers/clark.html

[5]   Ibid.

[6]   Tarjanne, Dr. Pekka, "Welcoming Address for INTERNET@TELECOM95 Conference-Secrtary General, International Telecommunication Union," Geneva, Switzerland, October 7, 1995,
        http://ww3.itu.ch/TELECOM/pressdocs/papers/intern-e.html.

[7]   Cerf, Vint, "Keynote Address at Internet@Telecom95," Geneva, Switzerland, October 8, 1995,
        http://www3.itu.ch/TELECOM/pressdocs/papers/cerf.html

[8]   Ibid.

[9]   "HP, Five Paces, SecureWare to offer total Internet Banking Solution," SecureWare Press Release,
        http://www.sware.com/whatsnew/pressrelease/120495.html

[10]   Violino, Bob, "Internet Insecurity: Your Worst Nightmare," *Information Week,* February 19, 1996, pp. 34-36.

[11]   "HP, Five Paces, SecureWare to Offer Total Internet Banking Solution," SecureWare Press Release,
        http://www.sware.com/whatsnew/pressrelease/120495.html

[12]   Merel, Peter, "Consultation Paper on the Regulation of Online Information Services," July 7, 1995,
        http://www.usyd.edu.au/~pete/cprely.html

[13]   Ibid.

[14]   Booker, Ellis, "Early Adopters: The Lessons Learned," Press Clippings, *WEBWEEK,* November 27, 1995.

[15]   Ibid.

INDEX